ALSO BY SIMON DOONAN

Nasty:
My Family and Other Glamorous Varmints

Wacky Chicks:
Life Lessons from Fearlessly Inappropriate
and Fabulously Eccentric Women

Confessions of a Window Dresser:
Tales from a Life in Fashion

ECCENTRIC GLAMOUR

CREATING AN
INSANELY MORE FABULOUS YOU

SIMON DOONAN

PHOTOGRAPHS BY
ROXANNE LOWIT

SIMON & SCHUSTER
New York   London   Toronto   Sydney

Simon & Schuster
A Division of Simon & Schuster, Inc.
1230 Avenue of the Americas
New York, NY 10020

First Simon & Schuster hardcover edition April 2008

SIMON & SCHUSTER and colophon are registered trademarks
of Simon & Schuster, Inc.

For information about special discounts for bulk purchases,
please contact Simon & Schuster Special Sales at 1-800-456-6798
or business@simonandschuster.com.

Designed by Suet Y. Chong

Manufactured in the United States of America

1   3   5   7   9   10   8   6   4   2

Library of Congress Cataloging-in-Publication Data
Doonan, Simon
Eccentric glamour : creating an insanely
more fabulous you / Simon Doonan.
p.   cm.
Includes bibliographical references and index.
1. Women—Psychology. 2. Women—Attitudes.
3. Beauty, Personal. 4. Feminine beauty (Aesthetics).
5. Self-esteem in women. 6. Body image in women. I. Title.
HQ1206.D664 2008
646.7'0420207—dc22   2007032564

ISBN-13: 978-1-4165-3543-0
ISBN-10:   1-4165-3543-8

All photography copyright © Roxanne Lowit
except Malcolm Gladwell, page 138.
Illustration by Ruben Toledo, page 74.
Jacket illustration by Simon Doonan

This book is dedicated to the memory of all the crazy broads and blokes who have flung themselves off the ramparts of eccentric glamour, metaphorically or literally, including, but not limited to, Isabella Blow, Marc Bolan, Leigh Bowery, the Marchesa Casati, Nancy Cunard, Frances Faye, Wallace Franken, Rudi Gernreich, Radclyffe Hall, Jimi Hendrix, Brian Jones, Janis Joplin, Pepper LaBeija, Steven Robinson, Millicent Rogers, Edie Sedgwick, Stephen Tennant, Vita Sackville-West, and Mae West.

ACKNOWLEDGMENTS

Thanks to all the glam eccentrics who have provided the inspirational gasoline to this project, especially the ones who submitted to interrogation: Iris Apfel, Mickey Boardman, Hamish Bowles, Beth Rudin DeWoody, Amy Fine Collins, Malcolm Gladwell, Iman, Alexandra Jacobs, Lucy Liu, Tilda Swinton, Dita Von Teese, Isabel Toledo, Kelly Wearstler, and Lynn Yeager.

Thanks to Howard Socol and all my colleagues at Barneys who enthrall me with their varying degrees of glamour and eccentricity on a daily basis.

Thanks to the folks at the *New York Observer*, and Simon & Schuster, especially Amanda Murray and Tracey Guest. Thanks to Tanya McKinnon, James Addams, Robert Forrest, Albert Sanchez, Aaron Sciandra, and Jerry Stafford for their glamorous enabling.

Special gratitude to Roxanne Lowit, without whose photographs this book would be less glamourously eccentric. And thanks to Roxanne's incredibly patient assistant, Shoko Takayasu.

Finally, and most important, I want to thank Jonathan Adler, my dreamboat, my rock, the love of my life.

CONTENTS

CONTENTS

CONTENTS

CONTENTS

INTRODUCTION

Why the hell wouldn't you want to be one of the fabulous people, the life enhancers, the people who look interesting and smell luscious and who dare to be gorgeously more fascinating than their neighbors?

I recently left my apartment dressed as Queen Elizabeth II. Not queen as in corgis and tweed skirts, but queen as in decked out like a giant flashing Christmas tree on the occasion of some totally major state dinner. Accessories? Just a few: long white gloves, two rhinestone necklaces, eleven bracelets, three brooches, six rings, a sash, two dangly earrings, three medals, a hubcap-sized tiara, and a giant pair of bifocals.

As I rode down in the elevator on that sunny spring Saturday afternoon, I braced myself for the inevitable catcalls and vulgar badinage that common sense told me would erupt as soon as I appeared in the busy lobby of my Greenwich Village apartment building. Hopefully I would be able to hail a cab and flee before some random passerby elected to throw a half-eaten Big Mac at Her Majesty.

Why, you may well ask, had I made myself vulnerable to public humiliation in such a specific manner? All such questions will be answered when you read Chapter 12 of the style manifesto which you are holding in your hot little hands. For the moment, I would like to stay focused on the specific sequence of events that was about to occur.

Ping. The doors opened. I began to traverse the carpeted lobby deploying the measured, flat-footed gate of Her Majesty Queen Elizabeth II, which is very easy to imitate but nonetheless won Helen Mirren an Oscar, and might have done the same for me had I been given a crack at the role.

My doorman approached. I dropped my front door key into my white purse, clicked it shut and tried to look regal. I waved. He did not wave back.

He came out from behind his little desk and blocked my path.

(Cricket sounds.)

I looked at him. He looked at my tits. I looked at his eyes looking at my tits. My tiara flashed in the afternoon sunlight, causing him to wince.

I stood my ground and returned his stare.

It was hard to get a read on his expression. Was he about to call the co-op board? Had he already pressed a concealed button summoning men in white coats from Bellevue?

(More crickets.)

Finally he spoke. "Do you want your mail now," he asked, "or when you come back?"

(Abrupt cessation of crickets.)

I was too stunned to respond.

I was completely overcome by the profound, global, philosophical, and far-reaching significance of this surreal little moment and the thunderbolt of immediate but deep understanding it had afforded me.

In an instant I understood the utter pointlessness of ever being self-conscious, the utter pointlessness of restraint or

xiv

"good taste," the utter pointlessness of *not* having fun with one's personal style. I had left my apartment dressed as the reigning monarch of my birthplace, and my doorman seemed not even to have noticed. I now understood the futility of a life spent asking, "Does my bum look big in this?" Clearer than ever, I saw the pointlessness of a life lived without a dab of daring panache. I understood the role of eccentric glamour.

Eccentric glamour! Create it. Grab it. Feel it. Be it, and do so knowing that, even if you walk down the street wearing a gold leotard with your lesbian aunt Sylvia's mauve nylon fanny pack cinching your midriff, nobody is judging you. Some people may not even notice you. *Most people will be enjoying you.*

Eccentric glamour is your birthright and that of every woman—and a man or two. Claim it! Own it! As a glamorous eccentric you have carte blanche to do whatever the hell you want. Experiment! If I can leave my apartment in full queen drag and barely raise an eyebrow, then surely you are free to make a complete spectacle of yourself in any manner you see fit.

What is eccentric glamour?

Let me answer that question with another question: What is glamour?

Glamour is that mysterious, shimmering you-know-it-when-you-see-it quality that surrounds those who stand out from the crowd. A wicked combo of cheeky attitude and stylistic innovation, real glamour is always exhilarating and never pedestrian.

One way to get to the heart of the matter is to dissect four contemporary pairings: Mr. and Mrs. Clinton, Paris and Nicole, Posh and Becks, and Miss Piggy and Kermit.

Has gobs of glamour: Bill Clinton, Nicole Ritchie, David Beckham and Miss Piggy.

Has less glamour than partner: Hillary Clinton, Paris Hilton, Victoria Beckham, and Kermit.

As is immediately apparent from my analysis, glamour is inextricably bound up with intelligence, humor, and/or accomplishment. Bill and Nicole win out over Hillary and Paris because they are smarter and more fun. David Beckham radiates more glamour than his missus because of his godlike athletic prowess. Miss Piggy and Kermit? Sometimes all you need is a few French phrases and an unassailable belief in your own innate fabulousness.

And what about eccentric glamour?

Eccentric glamour—Miss Piggy is, by the way, the overall winner in this category—is an invigorating mixture of the expected and the unexpected, the habitual with the kooky, the constant and the kapow!

The basic elements of your personal style are important. Let's call them your style constants. Whether it's a glossy jet-black ponytail, a saucy beauty mark, a nuclear explosion of natural red curls, or a penchant for livid green tango shoes, every gal needs a repertoire of well-chosen style constants. Simultaneously communicating and defining your unique identity, these signature flourishes are your own personal station identification. Unaffected by fleeting trends or the whims of fashion, your style constants are the glamorous foundations that will remain with you through thick and thin (literally and figuratively).

So where does the eccentricity come in?

Now take your style constants—those unique gestures which your fans and friends have come to associate so strongly with you—and punctuate them with a spontaneous gesture, a jolt of the unexpected, a rhinestone bucket bag, a pair of mariachi slacks, a vintage Pucci poncho. Et voilà! Eccentric glamour is the happy result.

Do today's celebs possess eccentric glamour? The answer is, for the most part, a giant, resounding *no!* Red-carpet glamour is, as I will prove to you repeatedly in the upcoming pages, the antithesis of eccentric glamour. Hiring a stylist who scrounges free frocks on your behalf from top designers does not really qualify as "creative expression." And today's celebs are, for the most part, much too chicken, too risk averse, too scared of that what-were-they-thinking page in *Star* magazine to indulge in eccentric glamour. Naughty, boring, conformist celebs!

As must already be apparent, the book you are clutching is by no means a typical style advice book. There are no before-and-after pictures or snappy lists or kicky bullet points. My methods are circumlocutive, to say the least.

On the following pages you will find a mixture of cultural commentary and personal disclosure, generously seasoned with gushings of wildly dictatorial and reckless style advice. Caution: These provocative tips should not be followed like a recipe. Developing a sense of eccentric glamour means taking your own path. My role is to mix up the signposts and start you on your journey.

Not sure which direction to take? No problem. As you will see in Chapter 1, I have invented a whole new system to guide your through the labyrinth of stylistic self-discovery. According to my theory, there are three types of glamorous eccentric: the Socialite, the Existentialist, and the Gypsy. In these three broad and inclusive categories you will find your eccentrically more glamorous self, you will find the means for self-reinvention, you will find the wherewithal to *say no to ho!* and resist the tidal wave of porno chic that threatens to engulf Western civilization.

In addition, these pages are liberally, randomly, and spontaneously larded with autobiographical humiliations and obsessions, including, but not limited to, my obsession with jazzercize and my forays into celebrity impersonation. It is my sincere wish that these tales from my own grody-to-szhooshy odyssey will entertain you as you undertake yours. For additional inspiration, my scribblings are evenly sprinkled with one-on-one interviews with some the world's most glamorous eccentrics, not including Isabella Blow. This legendary, deceased fashion muse is honored in a postscript musing.

Those of you who have enjoyed stories about my early years in my *New York Observer* columns and previous books will be happy to know that the dramatis personae of my wacky childhood—key figures in the evolution of my beliefs regarding eccentric glamour—are omnipresent.

"A life of eccentric glamour seems like a lot of hard work," I already hear you kvetch. Good point. Why not wear a muumuu and flip-flops, grab a bag of Doritos, and watch the parade from the sidelines?

First, evolving your own brand of eccentric glamour is good for your psyche. Knowing who you really are and dressing the part—with an air of amused recklessness—is life affirming for you and life enhancing for other people. When the eccentrically glamorous you walks down the street, whether you are a wiry Italian greyhound or a lovable lumbering labradoodle, you will feel gorgeously empowered and you will fill your neighborhood and workplace with positive vibrations. Think of it as a civic duty of sorts.

Second, it's creatively fulfilling. Constructing and designing a glamorously eccentric you means understanding and magnifying the core of your individuality. Your clothing represents a challenging and groovy canvas for self-expression. While the typical TV boobs 'n' Botox 'n' bleach makeovers force every woman to look the same—see *The Real Housewives of Orange*

County—the transformations I strive to provoke in this book are the very opposite. Honing your style constants, developing a glamorously eccentric look is a creatively and psychologically satisfying process because it involves revealing and magnifying everything that is unique and idiosyncratic about you. Follow my dictates and you will end up looking like nobody else on the planet, give or take a tiara or two.

Third, why the hell wouldn't you want to be one of the fabulous people, the life enhancers, the people who look interesting and smell luscious and dare to be gorgeously more fascinating than their neighbors?

Now grab my hand. Let us walk together into this brave new world of eccentric glamour where conformity is the only crime and dressing down is the only faux pas.

CHAPTER 1

Simone de Beauvoir Was Totally Hot

Say no to ho and yes to eccentric glamour

You run into an old acquaintance. You are unable to recall her name. It might be Eva, or maybe Yvonne. You're not quite sure.

You take a closer look. Yes, it's definitely Eva, but she is barely recognizable. Eva has undergone some kind of grotesque transformation. She used to look a bit like Melanie Griffith in *Working Girl*. Now, thanks to her fake hair extensions, fake nails, fake spray tan, fake collagen lips, and fake boobs, she looks like a cross between Britney Spears, Mrs. Gastineau (the mother), and a blow-up doll.

Somehow you manage to refrain from asking her why she no longer looks like a librarian and is now dressing like a porno star, and you say, "Goodness me! Don't you look . . . stunning! No, I mean it . . . I'm totally stunned."

Delicately inserting a fake nail into the corner of her fake mouth to extract a couple of errant strands of fake hair—hair that was previously dark brown and, until recently, belonged to a disadvantaged miss on a faraway continent—Eva tells you she's decided to "go for *the natural look.*"

Yes, you heard right. She said "the natural look."

Sheesh! Times have changed.

Once upon a time, the natural look meant Joan Baez or Ali MacGraw or the thin, pretty one from The Mamas and the Papas, or, for that matter, dear old Mama Cass herself. Bohemian, groovy, and eccentric, a natural gal was a love child, a hippie, a free spirit whose idea of dressing up for a big night out in Haight-Ashbury was to shove a daisy in her hair and dab a bit of patchouli on one of her salient features.

Now, apparently, it means looking about as natural as The Lady Bunny.

As shocking as Eva's transformation is, you cannot shake the feeling that she looks hauntingly familiar.

Yes! Open the window and stick your head out. Heavens to Betsy! There are identical Eva clones strutting through every shopping mall. Embracing "the natural look" has, in fact, become something of an epidemic.

Many of your peers have opted—with the help of liposuction, collagen, and a great deal of sass—for the Eva route. They have said yes to ho, and as a result they now resemble a bunch of aging Bratz dolls. That boobs 'n' bleach 'n' Botox makeover is standard for any woman seeking to reinvent herself. This look is part of the I-don't-want-to-look-like-a-grown-up-anymore-but-I-do-want-to-look-like-my-daughter-who-just-happens-to-dress-like-a-hoochie-dancer movement.

"What's so wrong with dressing supersexy?" I hear you ask.

"Are you some freaky middle-aged prude?" I also hear you ask.

Call me crazy, but I believe that there might just be more to being a woman than prancing around dressed up like a Stepford blow-up doll. *Non?* In my experience you gals are highly idiosyncratic creatures whose true essence is riddled with subtlety and nuance. Your sizzling sexuality is only one aspect of a complex and intriguing picture.

Let me digress briefly to clarify my position on the subject of vulgarity. Simply put, I adore it! A dash of bad taste is a vital component of eccentric glamour. I realize this may sound a little contradictory: On the one hand I am inveighing against an overtly whorish look that has regrettably become the chosen makeover option for so many women; on the other hand I am extolling the virtues of vulgarity. What gives? Yes, ho style is vulgar, but it is not the vulgarity per se against which I inveigh. It is the conformity. It is the Stepford factor. It is the lack of personal expression. It is the fact that this hideous epidemic of blow-up dolls is compromising the ability of American women to develop an eccentrically glamorous individual style.

There is nothing wrong, I hasten to add, with maximizing one's physical appeal, but there is a difference—*vive la différence!*—between being alluring and dressing like a ho. Or, as Oscar Wilde might have put it were he alive today, "To expose one cleavage seems unfortunate. To expose both cleavages seems like carelessness."

Eccentric glamour—something Mr. Wilde, with his velvet knickers and floppy foulards, had in spades—is your only defense against the tidal wave of dangling pasties, lady lumps, hoochie hot pants, and skanky halter tops. With a missionary zeal, I implore you gals to seek out eccentrically glamorous alternatives to the ubiquitous cheapness and tackiness that currently pass for personal style. Remember that porno chic is an evil conformist trend that has the potential, if allowed to burgeon unchecked, to eclipse individuality and personal eccentricity. So banish the badonkadonkdonk!

Say no to ho!

Let's go grab Eva right now, shake some sense into her, and put her on the righteous path to eccentric glamour.

Oh! Too late!

We missed our opportunity. She's jumped up on a table out of earshot, and she's doing the watusi.* She jiggles. She wiggles. She giggles.

As you observe your old pal, you start to feel a bit left out. There she is clutching a large blue umbrella drink and getting her ass pinched, and she was always the designated driver, the sensible one who stood on the sidelines at the office party! There's no denying she looks like a big whore, but she's just having so much fun that it's hard not to feel a teensy bit envious. And that butt-crack tattoo—apparently she had it done down in Miami when she was rat-faced drunk—is certainly getting her lots of attention, despite the adjacent lipo scars.

Being in Eva's orbit is having an odd effect on you. As much as you might be completely dumbfounded by her unquestioning embrace of porno-chic, this encounter with your old pal is making you feel frumpy and frowzy and uninteresting. She may be one of the hos, but you are one of the schlumps, which is infinitely more depressing. You are suddenly seized with the desire to deschlump and reinvent yourself. Tired of playing Agnes Gooch, you decide you want a slice of the action. And why not? Everybody else is doing it, why not you?

We are living in an age where makeovers and boob jobs are as common as cheeseburgers. "Beauty" is no longer just for celebs; it's now a commodity that can be bought at the mall or the dermatologist with a flick of your credit card. Transfor-

---

* Readers who crave a more in-depth understanding of the porno-chic phenomenon should read *Female Chauvinist Pigs* by Ariel Levy.

mation is the *mot du jour*. You can't turn on the telly without confronting images of blubbering former "ugly ducklings" reunited with their disbelieving families.

So why not you?

A large question mark or two appears over your head.

Do you have what it takes to reinvent yourself?

The answer, of course, is a resounding YES!

But do you have what it takes to reinvent yourself without following in Eva's footsteps? Do you have what it takes to resist the pressures to conform to the new slutty norm?

Can you figure out how to unearth and release the self-invented, nonconformist, taboo-busting individual who lurks inside you—and inside every woman, and certain types of men—and dive into a sparkling lagoon of style and fashion without ending up looking like a tramp?

The answer to all your questions is resting in your hot little hands.

Before you commission that boob lift and reach for the bleach, you must read this chapter and read it good. I wrote it with the sole purpose of stemming the tidal wave of Evas. My goal is to show the women of America that there is another way!

Gypsies, Existentialists, and Socialites— The Three Roads to Eccentric Glamour

In order to reinvent herself, a gal needs a concept.

If you are looking to reimagine your personal style, you cannot simply head for the local mall and start shopping your brains out. You need a good, strong, viable idea. A framework. Without it you will flounder about and, because it is the prevailing style, you will end up adopting Eva's trampy look.

Embracing the life of a glamorous eccentric is easier than

you would imagine. The choices are not infinite. When the chips are down, there are, you will be delighted to learn, only three roads that lead to the kingdom of eccentric glamour: Gypsy, Existentialist, and Socialite.

At first this might sound utterly demented and insanely limited. It's not. It is, as you will see, merely a fact of life.

The Gypsy is the ethereal, poetic, crafty, artsy, bohemian face of eccentric glamour. Though stylish, she privileges sensuality, freedom, and comfort over fashion. Think Julia Roberts in her current mom-living-at-the-beach mode.

The Existentialist is infinitely more severe, dramatic, graphic and intellectual than her wayward Gypsy sister. While the Gypsy is all about the flesh, the Existentialist is all about the mind. Think edgy. Think beatnik. Think Annie Lennox or Chrissie Hynde.

The Socialite is heavy on the gloss, light on the eccentricity. She radiates old-school glamour. She's lacquered, designer clad, high heel addicted, manicured, elegant, and slightly bitchy. Though more "normal" in her appearance than both the Gypsy or the Existentialist, the Socialite compensates with an irreverent and sparkling wit. She is, in many ways, the conventional center of the spectrum, flanked on either side by the Gypsy and the Existentialist. Think Anna Wintour. Think Jackie O.

Et voilà!

A Gypsy, an Existentialist, or a Socialite? Take your pick.

There is no need to feel pigeonholed or confined by these three categories. Within each group there are, as you will see, endless nuances and permutations that allow for unlimited personal expression.

Some of you will find that you are a combo platter—the Socialite/Existentialist is, for example, an unexpected and growing phenomenon—and a small number of you will bounce around effortlessly among all three. Such people are rare and often unusually creative: interior designers Celerie Kemble and Kelly Wearstler spring easily to mind. The world's best-known Gypsy/Existentialist/Socialite amalgam is, however, a fashion model. Two words: Kate Moss.

Eight A.M.: Kate skips through British customs after a sun-drenched Saint Barth's photo shoot, looking every inch the bedraggled, bohemian Gypsy in denim hot pants, minicaftan, and embroidered pashmina.

Lunchtime: there's Kate in a quirky black Marc Jacobs or Balenciaga ensemble—knee-high black boots, opaque black tights, minikilt, military-style fitted jacket—having an Existentialist chat and a pint of beer with an enigmatic musician friend in an Islington pub.

As the sun sets, La Moss is snapped vamping off to some fancy opening on the arm of Karl Lagerfeld in vintage bijoux and a Chanel gown looking every inch the groovy Socialite.

Miss Moss is unusual. You may eventually skip around like the stylishly louche Kate, but for now let us concentrate on finding your home base, your style identity. Let's find the best fit for your personality.

And, if you really are a total tramp whose main ambition in life is to lap-dance every bloke within screeching distance, then feel free to embrace porno-chic and continue dressing the part. Best of luck! May God go with you. Those of you who are looking to express the full majesty of your essence via your personal style, please read on.

The Gypsy

Are you a hazy, lazy, rustic, poetic, ethereal free spirit? Or maybe you always wanted to be but were too scared to let loose in case you ended up going berserk on LSD and jumping out of a window. Have you always wondered what a hash brownie tastes like but never dared to look up a recipe online in case you end up on some kind of FBI list?

If you always fancied yourself as a bit of a hippie but were terrified to go for it, you may be a repressed Gypsy, a Gypsy manqué. Now is the time to find your inner Janice and let her rip.

There is much to recommend the Gypsy lifestyle.

First, it's incredibly romantic. Imagine yourself living in a yurt or, better yet, a bedouin tent. Imagine calling your children in to dinner by banging a beribboned tambourine on your hip.

Gypsy style affords carte blanche not found in the structured, uptight world of the Socialite. You can be wild. You can be Carmen. You can be tempestuous. While Existentialist chicks feel obliged to imbue everything with solemnity and meaning, you Gypsies can shriek and bite the air—*raaar!*—just because you feel like it. You can be uninhibited. Imagine yourself whirling around a campfire in a flounced cheesecloth skirt, flashing your eyes, not to mention those vintage embroidered Victorian bloomers you found at the flea market, at a group of swarthy adoring monosyllabic blokes with gold teeth. What could be more dreamy?

Having generalized and hyperbolized about the Gypsy, let me try to be a little more helpful. Though freedom, comfort, and sensation are key components, the Gypsy lifestyle is more than just a rehash of groovy '60s counterculture ideas. Within this group there are endless variations and genres. Here are four of my personal favorites:

The Euro-glam Gypsy

A throwback to the YSL rich hippies of the early 1970s—think Marisa Berenson or Talitha Getty— the Euro-glam Gypsy is a show-off who loves ethnic fabrics, finger cymbals, appliqués, rickrack, and fringe. Her idea of heaven is to be shot for *Vogue* while getting her hands hennaed by a leathery-faced crone in some far-flung, hectic marketplace. A celebrity example? Jade Jagger is the contemporary queen of the Euro-glam Gypsies. The daughter of Mick and Bianca has built a whole brand identity simply by floating about her house in Ibiza rimming her eyes with kohl and festooning her walls with sari fabrics.

While the Euro-glam Gypsy is at great pains not to appear wealthy or bourgeois—in sharp contrast to the Socialite who, as you will see, often does the complete opposite—she usually has a bit of money tucked away. Fashion models often become Euro-glam Gypsies when they pass their sell-by date: '90s glamazons Marpessa and Helena Christensen are good examples. These gals have accumulated the kind of shekels needed to bankroll the indolent Euro-glam Gypsy lifestyle.

What does she wear? At the time of writing, Matthew Williamson and Duro Olowu are the Euro-glam Gypsy's favorite designers. A major flea market hag, she is always scouring the stalls for a vintage Ossie Clarke or Thea Porter or Zandra Rhodes.

Is she loyal to this style?

Yes, emphatically, yes! Once a Euro-glam Gypsy, always a Euro-glam Gypsy. These gals are lifers. Though she may tidy herself up for funerals and court appearances, it is almost unheard-of for a Euro-glam to become a Socialite. This would involve having her tattoos removed and bidding adieu to all her friends, freaks, and acquaintances.

The Isadora Gypsy

The Isadora Gypsy is named after Isadora Duncan, that fabulously crazy chick who, at the beginning of the last century, leaped around barefoot in the dirt waving a piece of chiffon and, as a result, invented the concept of modern dance.

Like her namesake, the Isadora Gypsy has a strong theatrical sense and loves dressing up: She wears panne velvet and vintage lace and medievalish robes and turbans a la Edith Sitwell. She adores massive rings, beading, and dévorée velvet. Her dream is to find a vintage Fortuny frock at Goodwill. The fact that this will never happen feeds her overall sense of romantic disappointment.

Regarding her psyche: The Isadora Gypsy is more cultured, better educated, and less trendy than her Euro-glam sister. Virginia Woolf is her favorite writer, olive green is her preferred hue. As a result, she is prone to bouts of melancholy. She does not have the reservoirs of happy superficiality that keep the Euro-glam Gypsy shrieking with laughter 24/7. While the Euro-glam is knocking back champagne at Art Basel in Miami, the Isadora Gypsy is far more likely to be found contemplating the translucency of an art nouveau vase on the Portobello Road or weeping quietly in the corner of Vita Sackville-West's all-white garden in Sussex, England.

(If you decide, upon reading this, that this is who you really are, you may want to leaven the steady diet of Virginia Woolf with a little distracting Candace Bushnell, just to mix things up a little and keep the blues at bay.)

Contemporary celebrity example? The majority of Hollywood actresses stick with a Socialite wardrobe. If they ever dare dabble in Existentialist or Gypsy style, they are massacred by the tabloids and hurled onto the what-was-she-thinking page. (See Björk the Existentialist.) There are a couple of exceptions: Cate Blanchett and Tilda Swinton have an Isadora/Existentialist thing going on, which makes them the darlings of the high-fashion monde.

Caution: The Isadora Gypsy is accident prone. She is quite likely to drown while having an Ophelia moment in a fast-running stream, or, lke the original Isadora, get throttled when her trailing scarf gets caught in the wheels of her sports car. Her death, though often unexpected, is never mundane.

The Green Gypsy

If sustainability and fair trade are more important to you than Gypsy glamour—i.e., you prefer hemp flip-flops over towering espadrilles by Christian Louboutin—you may well be a Green Gypsy.

Formerly known as the Birkenstock Gypsy, the Green Gypsy is a fast-growing category in Hollywood. Inspired by Green celebs like Leo and Brad, more and more young lasses—think Kate Hudson, think Liv Tyler—are looking for environmentally responsible, organic garments. Especially if they are knocked up or just hanging out at their ten-million-dollar Malibu beach shacks.

Warning: Just because a garment is made of organic cotton does not mean it has the allure and the sizzle that are part and parcel of the eccentric glamour lifestyle. Try to be ruthlessly objective when buying and accessorizing green garments. Do not sacrifice style for sustainability. At the end of the day, a burlap tabard is just . . . a burlap tabard. Unless you team your tabard with a pair of cruelty-free Stella McCartney black patent spikes, you run the risk of looking as if you are an extra in a suburban dinner theater production of *The Canterbury Tales*.

Psych alert: While the Euro-glam Gypsy tends toward superficiality, the Green Gypsy, with her solar panels, her malfunctioning compost toilet, and her constant anxieties about the size of her carbon footprint, is crucifyingly earnest. If you enter this category, please try not to become a dogmatic bore.

The Hollywood Gypsy

The patron saint of Hollywood Gypsies is Ali MacGraw. You thought I was going to say Stevie Nicks, didn't you? Miss Nicks, thanks to her love of floaty chiffon and unstructured choreography, is really more of an Isadora Gypsy.

The Hollywood Gypsy, as personified by Miss MacGraw, is the well-scrubbed Malibu version of Gypsy style. In her crisp white caftans and discreet jewelry, yoga-loving Ali is the acceptable face of hippie, a woman with alternative ideals, a sizable bank account, and no body odor or armpit hair.

As they age, these Hollywood Gypsies can sometimes become Socialites. This can elicit accusations of betrayal by the Green Gypsies who often work at the health food stores or yoga centers patronized by the Hollywood Gypsies.

Let's recap: Gypsy style is, as you can see, a colorful and seductive category. I predict that, after reading this chapter, a significant number of you readers will emerge as committed tambourine-banging glamorously eccentric Gypsies.

The biggest plus for Gypsies of all stripes? Gypsy style, in all its various manifestations, is a great look for larger girls.

Off-the-shoulder Carmen blouses, embroidered taffeta skirts, Victorian piano shawls, and espadrilles, while great on a skinny gal, also work wonders for the chunky glamorous eccentric. Gypsy clothing is not so much slimming as gorgeously distracting. Let me put it to you this way: When your clothing says, "I'm a flamboyant, vivacious, interesting person!" as opposed to the less appealing, "I'm a chubby person in dreary tentlike self-effacing clothes!" your universe can only change for the better.

Gypsy décor is similarly forgiving: It is by far the quickest and easiest to execute. Creating a gypsy lair is a total no-brainer. Any idiot can take a bunch of saris and staple them around a room. Any nitwit can make a room look fabulous by adding a couple of camel saddles. How much brainpower does it take to dangle a few dream catchers and sling a hammock or two across your living room? (Is this why so many fashion models favor this style *chez eux?*)

The biggest advantage of Gypsy décor is that there is no upkeep. It's a very unchallenging style, and once installed, the Gypsy abode requires no maintenance or cleaning whatsoever. While the Existentialist is constantly retouching that white floor, and the Socialite is flagellating herself with those what-would-Jackie-do comparisons, the Gypsy is gainfully occupied casting runes, playing her dulcimer, or generally flitting about.

And it's quick: While Socialite décor is all about painstakingly prissy precision and anal-retentive immaculate surfaces, Gypsy décor can be achieved in a matter of minutes just by hurling a few Himalayan rugs, alpaca throws, and exotically scented candles into a room.

The drawbacks: Gypsies are far more likely to have radon gas in their homes. This is simply because it would never occur to a Gypsy actually to test for radon.

Gypsies are tchotchkaholics. They tend to create an environment that looks like a Moroccan souk. As a result, visitors to a Gypsy cave are constantly picking things up and saying, "How much is this?" Entrepreneurial Gypsies are quite likely to start selling things. Others will find this mildly irritating.

Last but not least, because of the cluttered nature of their pads, Gypsies often find that people have been living with them for months and they never knew. For this reason, Gypsies are statistically much more likely to harbor felons, albeit unwittingly, than Socialites or Existentialists.

The Socialite

While it is undeniably true that Jackie Kennedy Onassis, Babe Paley, and CZ Guest are the primordial slime from which all subsequent Socialites emerged, today's Socialite is any gal—a manicurist, a celeb, a dog groomer, a bank manager, an anchor lady—who loves a well-cut skirt, a Chanel watch (real or fake), and a crucifyingly high heel. Today's Socialite can be highborn or common as muck.

This is good news for you, the ordinary woman on the street. You do not need money, power, or an obscenely rich husband in order to embrace the spiffy, manicured glam of Socialite style. Anyone can be a Socialite, even you, because Socialite is a state of mind.

Of all the three styles, the Socialite has the least amount of eccentricity. Her style, though culled from the latest fashion collections, has a classic panache. She herself is not particularly creative. She leaves that to the Puccis, Valentinos, Oscar de la Rentas, and Karl Lagerfelds of the world, or the knocker-offers thereof. She's a follower, not a leader.

But let's not be too hard on her: The Socialite is invariably a scintillating and idiosyncratic conversationalist. While she may lack daring in her wardrobe choices, the glamorously eccentric Socialite has a wicked wit. The humor, poise, and sizzling repartee of the practiced Socialite more than compensate for her low eccentricity score.

And here's the best thing about her, the Socialite is the world's leading patroness of la mode. Whether shopping at Strawberry or Chanel, she supports fashion designers by spending an enormous amount of money on clothing. And, as a bonus, she abhors the slutty ho trend. The Socialite attracts men by cultivating her allure, not by flashing her breasts or jumping in and out of chauffeured vehicles sans panties.

Despite the commitment to that old-school Jackie Kennedy manicured glamour, it would be a gigantic mistake to assume that white chicks have some kind of monopoly on Socialite style. The fact is that ladies of color constitute a huge chunk of the Socialite demographic. Please recall, dear reader, the incident where a certain black billionaire megastar/entrepreneur was banging on the door of the Hermès store in Paris at closing time. It's not just Oprah. A vaste number of African Americanas are motivated by the Socialite desire to look spiffy and nifty and swanky and turned out. The black Socialite wants to wear a Dolce & Gabbana suit with a white fox fur and a giant pair of Dior glasses, and who can really blame her? Socialite style, with its emphasis on polished designer glamour, makes perfect sense for an African-American chick from a hardscrabble background. Not every stylish black woman is a ghetto escapee, but the gal who is will always tend to recoil from the raggedy-ass hippie style of the Gypsy. Having seen more than her share of grunge, she finds it alien and annoying.

The Existentialist approach, as you will see, is just as irrelevant to the black Socialite as Gypsy style: Even though she might buy freaky artwork from an Existentialist artist, the black Socialite has zero interest in looking kooky or conceptual herself.

Celebrity examples? Mary J. Blige is a label-lovin' Socialite. So is Foxy Brown. So—when she's wearing her ladylike Marc Jacobs outfits—is Lil' Kim. Yes, ladies of color have the Socialite's unapologetic stop-at-nothing passion for designer clothing.

If I were a chick, I would probably dress Socialite, with a top note of Existentialist. Having been born into postwar austerity—I spent my early years in a two-room walk-up with no kitchen or bathroom—I share the Socialite's antipathy toward any style that disingenuously attempts to riff on downward mobility. Why dress poor if you are not? Why dress down when you can dress *up*?

Performing a colonoscopy? What to wear?

Skin tone aside, Socialite style is ultimately about confidence. Unlike the Existentialist or the Gypsy, the Socialite dresses to communicate power and competence and order. Socialite style is, therefore, the best style for professional women.

Let me rephrase that: Socialite style, with its carefully crafted cocktail of minimal eccentricity and designer fashion, is the *only* style for professional women.

Dressing for work has always been a minefield of complexity and symbolism. There is a codified language that changes from milieu to milieu. Fashion, your personal style, can either blast you through the glass ceiling or hurl you on the unemployment heap. Certain styles can annihilate credibility in some professional situations and enhance it in others.

For example: When a lady doctor is advancing upon you with a needle or a probe of any kind, you expect that person to be wearing clean, well-cut garments from the conservative end of the Socialite spectrum such as those designed by Ralph Lauren or Ann Taylor. A medical professional can destroy every ounce of confidence you have in her simply by wearing the wrong blouse or shoes. Nobody, and I really do mean nobody, wants a colonoscopy performed by an Existentialist lady in an avant-garde Comme des Garçons humpback dress. No gal in her right mind wants corrective eye surgery performed by a dirndl-wearing refugee from Haight-Ashbury. Gypsy and Existentialist are no-nos for health-care professionals.

The profession of law has similar constraints: Nobody wants his or her will drawn up by a Gypsy wearing armfuls of Morrocan bracelets and a plunging Roberto Cavalli leopard-print, silk-chiffon minicaftan.

The bottom line? Eccentricity must be kept at a minimum, or credibility will suffer. If your profession entails an iota of responsibility for the health or finances of others, you must minimize your visual quirks. You can freak out on your own time, but when you are at work you must adopt the Socialite style or die.

Dermatologists, it should be noted, have a little more carte blanche than other medics. The new emphasis on Botox and other cosmetic beauty procedures has dragged these gals out of the mundane world of ingrown hairs and pus-filled abscesses and into the stylish world of Lanvin and Prada.

Though still confined to the Socialite category, dermatologists can be a little more flamboyant and fashion forward than other professional chicks, without the loss of any credibility. A designer-clad derm—in this season's Vionnet or Ricci—is assumed to be a wealthy and therefore successful and therefore accomplished person. As a result, the top skin peelers in America—Dr. Pat Wexler, Dr. Lisa Airan et al.—frequently appear on the best-dressed lists alongside hard-core label-addicted Socialites like Marina Rust and Victoria Traina.

Yes, I said addicts.

Of the three groups—Existentialists, Gypsies, and Socialites—the Socialite is the most likely to develop a severe fashion addiction. (Gypsies, as you can well imagine, are associated with other types of addictions.)

Though crisp, clean, and unimpeachably chic, the Socialite cannot go for twenty-four hours without buying herself a new frock/bag/blouse/stiletto. She is an unapologetic label queen. If fashion was glue, every Socialite would be lying in the gutter like Laura Dern in that movie *Citizen Ruth*, desperately huffing her brains out. The Socialite is perpetually high on designer crack.

The level of fashion addiction may vary in degree, but there are a number of behavioral traits that are consistently found in all Socialites.

Ixnay on the Gypsies

Though socially adept, Socialites are not particularly comfortable around Gypsies. The worst thing that could happen to a Socialite is to be forced to live with a Gypsy. This would be the equivalent of asking Anna Wintour to live with Stevie Nicks. The smell of sage and the general sloppy unpredictability of her roommate would drive the *Vogue* editor in chief totally bonkers.

Socialites fare little better alongside Existentialists. Because they are disinterested in avant-garde fashion, Socialites find Existentialists bewildering and annoying. The Socialite is a Dior, Tuleh, Prada, Pucci, Chanel, Tory Burch, Blahnik, Ralph Lauren, Louboutin, Lilly Pulitzer kind of a gal. While Socialites believe that Paris is the fashion capital of the world, Existentialists are exclusively focused on Belgium, and occasionally England.

The fact that Brit designer Hussein Chalayan once buried his collection in his backyard for a few weeks, prior to showing it to the press, while delightful to the Existentialist, is appalling and horrible to the Socialite.

Miss Manners

Perpetually terrified that people will think she's an uptight bitch, the Socialite overcompensates wildly. Not only is she charming and funny, she is also surprisingly and effusively polite. Like the late neat freak Joan Crawford, she compulsively sends flowers and is quite capable of penning a thank-you note for a thank-you note.

Fairy wands

Socialites, it must be acknowledged, are invariably quite prissy. No Socialite would ever allow herself to have a cruddy bathroom. Furry toilets and moldy backsplashes, though part and parcel of the Gypsy lifestyle, are profoundly unacceptable to the Socialite.

Even the most quotidienne Socialite prefers to touch as few things as possible with her bare hands. This is why she puts Lucite wands on her drapes. God forbid she should have to touch anything as unworthy and lowly and disgusting as curtain fabric!

Allied to the wand, but no less important to the Socialite, is the extension. I refer to the telescopic doodad that adds several feet, and a great deal of savoir faire, to your cobweb remover or feather duster. Highly recommended for dwarf Socialites.

She can kick your ass

Don't let the old-fashioned politesse deceive you: The Socialite is tougher than you think. If an Existentialist PETA supporter hurls a soy-cream pie at her because she is wearing a chinchilla shrug, the Socialite is quite capable of slapping her attacker upside the head with her studded Fendi baguette.

The Existentialist

Existentialism, for the ignorant reader, was a philosophy developed by Jean-Paul Sartre in midcentury Paris. The basic idea was that life did not make any sense at all and that everything was chaotic and contingent. Insights into the utter meaninglessness of it all came in bursts of what Monsieur Sartre called *nausea*. Like most French people, Jean-Paul was something of a misanthrope, declaring famously that "hell is other people."

The Sartres, with their angrily belted outerwear and grumpy expressions, were not the most fun people on earth. They did, however, give birth to the beatniks, who begat all subsequent supercool, edgy style movements: punk, grunge, downtown chic, etc., etc. Even the black-clad fashionistas of the '90s owe their look to Jean-Paul and Simone. *Merci beaucoup!* This is the edgy, belligerent, provocative, creative, innovative face of eccentric glamour.

"What's so glamorous about smelly beatniks or menacing punk rockers?" I hear those readers of a more conventional Socialite orientation ask, to which I reply, "As per my introduction, any useful definition of the word 'glamour' now goes way beyond that boring gold standard of manicured beauty laid down by the original Hollywood studio dream factory during the last century. Yes, back in the day, Marilyn and Liz had glamour, but so did Gertrude Stein and JFK and Ernest Hemingway and Giacometti and Dorothy Parker."

Still not getting it? Don't reproach yourself. A large part of the glamour of glamour comes from its extreme elusiveness.

Now let's get back to those glamorous Existentialists.

Though the smallest group, the Existentialists are the most creative and eccentrically glamorous of the three categories. While the Socialite rarely instigates trends, the Existentialist does little else. She radiates edginess. While the Evas of this world adorn themselves for the delectation of the opposite sex, the Existentialist dresses for one person and one person only: herself.

Prominent Existentialists include Carine Roitfeld (editor in chief of French *Vogue*), Chrissie Hynde, and British art provocateur Tracey Emin.

There are no A-list celeb Existentialists. Jennifer Connolly and Charlotte Gainsbourg are about as close as it gets. Vanessa Paradis (Johnny Depp's crumpet)? She vacillates between Existentialist and Euro-glam Gypsy. The contemporary Hollywood red-carpet look is dominated by Socialite style—the antithesis of everything the Existentialist stands for.

She's an angry rebel who eschews the superficiality of contemporary culture. If she is unfortunate enough to catch any of the frothy fashion Oscar coverage on TV, the typical Existentialist experiences a strong desire to join the Taliban. If she were ever, by some bizarre serendipity, to find herself on the red carpet, and Joan Rivers asked her, "Who made your dress?" the Existentialist would either go into a tortured explanation of the designer's concept or shout, "Some poofter!" and keep walking.

Yes, Existentialists are a tad scary.

Gypsies are often frightened by them, and with good reason. While the good-humored Gypsy loves to run through the woods barefoot and sell toe rings to passing hikers, the Existentialist is busy on the shady side of the forest gathering poisonous mushrooms while plotting the overthrow of the government.

The Existentialist is very creative. Whether managing an art gallery or designing unbuildable buildings à la Zaha Hadid (a major Iraqi Existentialist), she is intent on using her provocative sensibility to change the world. While the Gypsy is sensual and organic and quite ditsy, the Existentialist is more rigid, intellectual, and Ayn Randian.

Don't worry, you don't have to be a rocket scientist to embrace your inner Existentialist. And you don't have to wear a monocle or become a German Expressionist–collecting lesbian. (But don't rule it out.)

Agonizing about whether or not you are an Existentialist is a bit of a waste of time. The truth of the matter is that you either are or you aren't. It is highly unlikely that you are a simmering Existentialist trapped in a Laura Ashley flounced frock. This does not mean that there is no volatility in this group. Some Existentialists transition out of this group as middle age looms: Courtney Love has made the switch from Existential style (wacky baby dolls and tiaras) to Socialite style (sleek designer gowns). Angelina Jolie is another example: She has relinquished her Goth garments and sadomasochistic styling in order—at the time of writing—to shill for the Socialite house of St. John knits!

Though society might discourage women from adopting the independent non-male-appeasing stance of the Existentialist, I do not. I positively insist on it. Even if you decide that you are a card-carrying Socialite, the unpredictability that is integral to the development of eccentric glamour definitely requires a soupçon of Existentialist style. Example: New York style icon Anne Slater—a beacon of Socialite style in her vintage Geoffrey Beenes and couture Ruccis—never leaves the house without her bizarre giant blue-tinted spectacles and massive Kazuko crystal bracelets.

Though it is a much more homogenous group than the Gypsies, Existentialist style can still be subdivided into four categories: Gamine, Gauche, Garçon, and Ghoul.

The Existentialist Gamine

This is the sweet face of Existentialism. She is Audrey Hepburn at the beginning of *Funny Face*, a bookworm in black ballet slippers, black turtleneck—the Existentialist style constant—and black toreador pants.

As with the other genres of Existentialist style, the Existentialist Gamine exudes intelligence. Her severe appearance suggests that she is interested in the world of philosophy and ideas while simultaneously challenging the self-indulgent glamour of Socialite style.

Note that I said "suggests." Herein lies the magic of the Existentialist style. It's the perfect combination of mystery and implied intellect. In other words: There's nothing quite like a black turtleneck to suggest an inner life, even where there may be none. The Existentialist Gamine is, therefore, a great look for gals like Paris Hilton who are perpetually accused of being dumb as planks and need to add a dash of gravitas to their image. Paris, if you are reading this, please stop dressing like an '80s bunny girl and give existential style a whirl.

The Rive Gauche Existentialist

The elder sister of the Gamine Existentialist, this is a great look for gals whose ripening figures no longer fit into those toreador pants.

Like Simone de Beauvoir and Simone Signoret, the Rive Gauche Existentialist is often named Simone, or maybe she has a weird spelling to her name. Cathy Horyn (note the spelling) of the *New York Times* is a great example of Rive Gauche Existentialist style. A beatnik and a thinker, she's severe, intimidating, and quite mysterious. In her black Lanvin trench coat and her Alaia leather kilt, she always manages to look like a member of the French Resistance.

While the Rive Gauche Existentialist's clothing is basic and simple, her hair is more complex: Cut à la Bettie Page, it features short, rounded bangs and shoulder-length side tresses. When she gets older she may go whole hog and wear it in a braid crown, a la Simone de Beauvoir, aka Mrs. Jean-Paul Sartre.

The Existentialist Garçonne

Courageous, self-invented women have always done it. Garbo did it in the '30s. So did Marlene. Punk girls did it in the 1970s. Pat Benatar did it in the 1980s. Madonna did it in the 1990s. I'm talking about boy chic. Butching it up. Dressing in drag. Suiting yourself.

F-to-M cross-dressing is strange and mysterious. The effect is not quite what you might expect. It would be logical to assume that the wearing of men's clothing might well detract from a gal's femininity. This is not always the case. It can often be the opposite. Elegant man drag, as worn by the ladies mentioned above, enhances rather than detracts from the femininity of the wearer.

For reasons too obvious to state, this Existentialist Garçonne look is big with certain gay women: Ellen is the big celebrity proponent of this style. Paradoxically, she looks much more girly in those nifty Sammy Davis Jr. suits of hers than she would if dressed in a ruched crepe de chine prom frock.

A tip for butch lesbians: Why do so many of you ladies, when faced with the compulsion to express your masculinity, opt for redneck/lumberjack style?

Girls! Instead of going whole hog and transforming yourself into an überbutch construction worker, why not play the Existentialist Garçonne? I for one would love to see more gay gals opting for Ellen's nifty tailored look. If I were a lesbian and I felt the inclination to butch it up a bit, I would like to think that I would adopt a dandified version of masculinity. Proustian fop, anyone?

Looking for a nonlesbian example of the Existentialist Garconne? Diane Keaton is single-handedly carrying the flag for this look among straight celebrity women. Her tailored English public school chic—more Waugh than Rat-Pack—is so at odds with the prevailing West Coast blow-up doll aesthetic that fashion pundits think she is insane and put her on those what-was-she-thinking? pages of the tabloids. Fortunately, she does not seem to care and continues to groove on her inner garçonne.

Vive La Keaton, the eccentrically glamorous Existentialist fashion rebel!

The Existentialist Ghoul

Paging Nina Hagen, Lene Lovich, and Siouxsie Sioux! Exene Cervenka! Ariella Up! Diamanda Galás! This is the most extreme genre of Existentialist. These are the kind of women who, in previous centuries, were burned at the stake.

Adopting this kind of scary look—Gothic maquillage, electrocution hair in vivid colors, historicist costume with sadomasochistic accessories—really limits your social interaction to those who are dressed exactly as you are and is therefore recommended only for the very young.

Existentialist Ghouls have become quite rare. At the time of writing, Amy Winehouse is the only contemporary example I am able to conjure. Only a genuinely unconventional gal can pull it off, and these are increasingly thin on the ground. I had high hopes for both Avril Lavigne and Ashlee Simpson. After a ballsy finger-throwing start to their careers, they both had Hollywood makeovers, revealing their innate conventionality in the process. It is my sincere hope that, with the writing of this book, I may prompt a few young ladies to follow La Winehouse—we're talking style, not self-destructive behavior—and take this courageous route.

Go Forth and Shop

Once you have designated yourself—Socialite, Existentialist, or Gypsy—all aspects of your life will become simpler. You will know not just which frocks to buy but also which scented candle or panty is the right one for you.

The whole process of shopping now becomes amusing and positively cinematic. In fact, you would do well to think of it as a movie production wherein you have two star credits: female lead and costume designer. You are Edith Head *and* Gloria Swanson. Having abandoned the role of insecure, nervous, sweaty ingénue, you are dressing an important star who has her own iconic look. Yourself!

You will be selecting garments that match your new sense of self. Your shopping trips will lose that dreadful disheartening random feeling. You will no longer be frantically chasing trends. You will no longer be making desperate attempts to understand the current fashion scene and see where you fit in. Instead you will be cherry-picking from the racks with a very specific mandate. And you will always find what you are looking for. The Gypsy/Existentialist/Socialite system of eccentric glamour is eternal. It's classic. While the fashion scene will always quiver, shift, and evolve, you will remain a constant: There will always be plenty of clothes for you.

Don't forget the *constant* and the *kapow*! As well as looking for new and innovative items—those unexpected jolts of style

I spoke about in my intro—be sure to stock up on those style constants that form the basis of your look.

Hey, Gypsy! When that appliquéd vintage dirndl skirt is too grody and stained to wear anymore, hit the flea market and find another. Or open your handbag and buy a new one from Miu Miu or Dries Van Noten. Your rottweiler ate your Peruvian poncho? No sweat. There're plenty more where that came from.

Hey, Socialite! Has your lavender shantung Prada brunch coat lost its je ne sais quoi? Replenish! Replenish! Replenish! Maybe a chartreuse Dior one this time?

Hey, Existentialist! Your black cashmere turtleneck has gone all nubby under the armpits. Guess what? They just got a new delivery at Uniqlo! Buy three and rotate them.

The best part about my method is that it gives you self-reliance. Once you have your category, you are set for life. No stylists or sycophantic designers for you! Even if you had the wherewithal to hire Rachel Zoe or L'Wren Scott, outsourcing the reinvention of your personal style is out of the question. A life of eccentric glamour means *you* expressing yourself, as opposed to *you* slavishly following the dictates of another human being.

This is not a burden. *Au contraire!* Eccentric glamour is a huge opportunity for creativity.

But be patient. Regardless of which style you adopt—Socialite, Existentialist, or Gypsy—it may take a while to hit your stride. Enjoy the ride. There is no rush. You are a work in progress.

Don't allow yourself to get disheartened. And above all, do not, as so many women today are doing, start gratuitously flaunting both your cleavages.

Say no to ho! Say yes to eccentric glamour!

*"The Highland Hospice charity shops
that dot every village in the north of Scotland
are where I live out my Miss Marple comes
to Warmington-on-Sea fantasies."*

TILDA SWINTON

Ethereal thespian, cinematic sensation, and fashion
muse responds to the Eccentric Glamour questionnaire.

What are you wearing?
One of my son's Aertex* shirts, his father's corduroy jacket, a
daisy chain, a Vivienne Westwood kilt, and no shoes.

**When did you first realize that you might in fact be a
glamorous eccentric?**
Putting a name to the condition: possibly only when you asked
me to participate in this folderol, but I did have an inkling fairly
recently at a Nine Inch Nails concert when I was stood on in
the mosh pit by a hobnail boot and realized that I had forgotten to change out of the toweling slippers from the hotel.

Were your parents horrified?
Given that my general father could chew the hind leg off

---

* Aertex: Aerated fabric often deployed in UK school uniforms.

Lesage* about the best ways to tissue-wrap gold frogging, I never reckoned they had a leg to stand on.

Are you prone to mood swings?
No, but don't tell anyone . . .

Have you ever been mocked for any of your glamorous eccentricities?
Naturally. Being broken into mockery at an early age by three brothers, I learned early to bear those wounds with great pride.

What is the most eccentrically glam thing in your closet?
Possibly a wool Hubert de Givenchy Pierrot dress—meaning it has a diamond print like a Pierrot costume—that is so lovely that even the fact that it reeks of mothballs—and could that be old lady pee?—won't stop me wearing it.

Have you ever wished you could trade in your life of glamorous eccentricity for one of dreary conformity?
No need to trade. I happily cultivate at least two entirely separate and distinct and yet mix 'n' match perfectly integrated lives. I'm finding it hard to work out which could best be described as glam eccentric and which dreary conformity. The Highland Hospice charity shops that dot every village in the north of Scotland are where I live out my Miss Marple comes to Warmington-on-Sea fantasies. Invariably more enticing in every way than the drudgery of the high chrome road.

When does eccentric glamour become idiocy?
When it is perpetrated with the aid of a solemn looking glass.

* Lesage: Legendary Paris-based house of couture beading and embroidery.

Who is your inspirational icon of glamorous eccentricity?
My fearless and sensationally chic (pronounced "chick") grandmother and my nine-year-old daughter.

Do men think you are hot?
Of course they do—whether they admit it or not.

**What is the thing that most offends your glamorously
eccentric sensibilities?**
The death knell: witless good taste.

Where do you wish to be buried, and in what?
In a shallow grave of sand, done up to the nines in a huge
flowery chiffon dress stretched out like a sail on a beach in the
Hebrides, pecked to pieces by birds.

CHAPTER 2

A Small Quantity of Spit

Guarding your self-esteem,
not to mention your maquillage

Ding-dong! It's 1963.

I am eleven years old and an Avon* lady is standing on our doorstep.

I stare at the Avon lady with a look of starstruck awe. I am delirious. I am beside myself. I have lived a life of quiet desperation, longing for this day. I've seen these women on TV and in my mother's magazines and dreamed of the day when one of them would ding-dong our front door, even though we have a door knocker.

These emissaries of beauty seem to me to exist on a mytho-

---

* Note to the good people of Avon and all their customers: The incident I am about to relate took place almost half a century ago and was, I am quite sure, far from representative. The Avon of today is a wonderful dynamic company deserving of nothing but unqualified respect. In other words, please don't sue me, good people of Avon. I would ask you instead to look upon this anecdote as a bit of glamorous and eccentric free promotion.

logical level. They are deities. They offer a promise of glamour to the unglamorous. What could be more godly than that? Like wandering apostles, the Avon ladies arrive uninvited at people's houses, bearing gifts and dispensing life-changing advice about beauty and skin care.

I am palpitating. My mother is already the most glamorous woman in our street. Imagine how insanely more fabulous she will be after getting beauty tips from a bona fide Avon lady!

Something about this Avon lady gives me pause. The middle-aged woman who is now standing before me, beads of sweat accumulating on her powdery mustache, looks nothing like the brittle beauties I have seen in the Avon ads. She is built more like a peasant laborer than a spokeslady.

I decide that this is a good thing. Even at this young age, and despite living in a household with two mentally ill people, I am a cockeyed optimist, especially when it comes to matters of beauty and style. Rather than be turned off by her appearance, I opt to see it as a positive indicator. Clearly this less than attractive Avon lady has been ordained because of her incredible expertise rather than her looks. It seems safe to assume that her beauty tips might be twice as magically effective as those dispensed by a more lovely Avon lady. At the end of the day, she's an Avon lady and that's good enough for me.

My mother Betty is in the kitchen. She is re-creating a recipe that she has clipped from a ladies' magazine. It seems to involve studding a large hunk of ham with a rainbow of fruits and vegetables using colored toothpicks.

Food is going through a very strange phase. Though the barbaric mudlike British cuisine is still the norm—shepherd's pie, bubble and squeak, gravy, overcooked greens etc.—Betty's magazines are making strenuous efforts to toss a bit of colorful joie de vivre onto the dreary postwar landscape. Vivid presentation and psychedelic garnishings are now de rigueur. Nothing emerges from Betty's kitchen without the addition of tinned pineapple chunks, chopped Jell-O, maraschino cherries, or sliced tomatoes. After years of being shot in black and white, food has now switched to Technicolor.

Though she does not yet know it, the same is about to happen to Betty.

"Mum, quick! It's urgent. A lady is here to see you!"

"Oh, Christ! Now what?"

Betty Doonan rolls her eyes, sighs, exhales, and puts down her cigarette. This entails placing the burning object not in an ashtray but rather standing it in the vertical Cape Canaveral position on the window ledge in front of the sink. Here it will slowly smolder until she comes back to reclaim it, or not.

This is a disastrous wartime habit, which Betty Doonan has never managed to kick, but it gives her the air of a film noir heroine. There is a rationale behind it. The vertical cigarette burns slower than one that is placed at the conventional forty-five-degree angle in an ashtray, allowing the smoker to extend its life span. Betty's complex life—working two jobs, cooking for lodgers and crazy relatives while maintaining a high quotient of eccentric glamour in her personal appearance—makes it extremely difficult for her to keep track of all these smoldering fags. As a result, they are to be found in every room. It is nothing short of a miracle that she has never burned the house down. This is due, no doubt, to the presence of flame-retardant chemicals in the filter.

In her white skirt, white blouse, and cork wedges, Betty, the only glamorous eccentric for miles, strides toward the front door. She has that God-I-hope-it's-not-the-police-calling-about-your-uncle-Dave-again look on her face.

The visitor is not a policeman. Betty is momentarily relieved.

"Afon callink!" pants the Avon lady in a voice that is the antithesis of American perkiness and reveals that she is not only winded but Polish.

"Can I help you?" says Betty, sounding slightly posh.

"No, but I sink I can help you," says the Avon lady with an air of confidence that takes Betty by surprise.

The Polish Avon lady begins her spiel. After a brief overview of the pure undiluted majesty that is Avon—all spoken in that deadpan Eastern European voice—the Avon lady begins to elaborate on Betty's shortcomings.

"Your makeup, she is very old hats," says the thickset visitor, sticking a large patent leather court shoe inside our front door. She is an imposing woman with a dramatic sweeping Carvel of champagne blond hair. She has elected to further compensate for her unfeminine physique by wearing a pink sweater set.

"Thanks a lot," says Betty Doonan loud enough so that my blind aunt Phyllis can hear. Phyllis often stands in the hallway and listens when Betty shoos away Jehovah's Witnesses or Boy Scouts. Occasionally a haunted-looking gypsy lady bangs on the door and tries to sell Betty clothespins. When Betty declines, the gypsy lady always curses her and spits into the privet hedge near the front gate.

Phyllis is always very amused by this. Phyllis is Betty's best friend and favorite lodger: Betty takes pleasure in entertaining her with her droll wit and her cheekiness.

"I vill update you and make you look like Leez Taylor."

Phyllis supresses a chuckle.

"I don't want to look like Liz Taylor," says my mother, who

spends a great deal of time and energy trying to look as much like Lana Turner as possible. Betty's look is pure 1940s. This is part of what makes her stand out from the other housewives. While all the other Doreens and Mabels are sporting the rococo perm of the 1950s—think Queen Elizabeth—Betty is still wearing her hair in the Bette Davis in *Now, Voyager* upward scroll. Impregnable to new trends, Betty has found a signature style and sworn allegiance.

Phyllis titters while toying with the ears of Lassie, her Seeing Eye dog. She is enjoying watching her bossy best friend being taken down a peg or two.

I am in full agreement with the Avon lady. It's the 1960s. It's time Betty started swinging and waved good-bye to her high hairdo. Some of my friends at school have commented unfavorably on my mother's overpainted Crawford lip line. It's time to get *with it.*

"I could do so much viz you . . . ," says the Avon lady coquettishly.

"I suppose so . . . ," says Betty with an unfamiliar compliant air.

"You shall have a *full consultation!*" says the Avon lady.

I jump up and down with excitement.

We all repair to the living room where the light is deemed to be optimal for Betty's transformation.

Panting heavily, the new arrival removes her pleated rain hood and plastic raincoat and hands them to my mother with a regal air.

The Avon lady looks around our living room as if inspecting a crime scene or scouting location for a séance.

"Please lie down," she says, pointing to an armchair, and we realize that what she actually meant to say was, "Please sit down." Aunt Phyllis giggles audibly and picks up her knitting.

Betty sits, crosses her legs, of which she is justifiably proud, and adjusts her bracelets. An air of tentative anticipation lights up her face. The Avon lady pulls up an occasional table, whirls a protective plastic cape around Betty, and begins to unpack her various products and applicators.

"First let me give you some advice from zuh heart," she says, adopting a tone of momentous woman-to-woman sincerity. "Never ever never leave ze house wizzout ze pancake!"

"Oh, no! I never wear pa—"

"Call me Irene," says the Polish Avon lady, pronouncing it "eye-ree-knee," as she begins sponging thick pancake of a tangerine hue onto Betty's face and neck. She uses a vigorous smearing motion that distorts Betty's face.

My sister and I begin to titter.

Lassie thinks the Avon lady might be harming Betty and lets out a few barks.

"Vatch it!" says Irene to all three of us. She seems to have no fear of large dogs, or anything else, for that matter. She forbids us to look or comment until the whole transformation is complete. We bury our heads in Lassie's fur.

"Much better!" says Irene, leaning back to admire her handiwork, "Your skin vaz pale. You need ze warmth. Now something for attracting ze mens! Rouge!"

The notion of combining orange pancake with a liberal application of red rouge seems daring and different. My anticipation grows.

Pale pink lips are applied. Betty normally wears red lips in the aforementioned film noir bow. This conceals that fact that her top lip is not quite as large as she might prefer it to be. Irene denounces this practice and informs Betty that from now on she will be following her God-given lip line.

"Now comes ze eyes," intones Irene, who keeps up a constant stream of commentary. Aunt Phyllis is knitting away and smiling from ear to ear. "Oh, I wish I could see what she's doing to you," she says.

"Me too," says Betty, who has twice attempted to look in the mirror but was forcibly restrained on both occasions.

"No yet," says Irene, who is sharpening her kohl pencil with a small Eastern European–looking penknife.

Betty normally accentuates her dark brown eyes with a softly applied pencil. I always admire the skill with which she blends and smudges the shadow around her deep eye sockets. I have watched her do this many times and looked forward to the day when I might give it a whirl on my own eyes.

Irene has a different approach. Having sharpened her kohl pencil to a brutal point, she begins to gouge it round and round Betty's eyes. The Liz Taylor/Cleopatra moment has arrived.

"That's a little painful," says Betty. Aunt Phyllis drops her knitting. My sister and I look at each other in shock. This is the first time any of us have ever heard my mother admit that anything caused her pain. She prides herself on her ability to rise above even the most extreme forms of physical discomfort. North Irish Betty always claimed that childbirth was not painful at all and that other women, especially Englishwomen, made far too big a deal about it.

"You must suffer if you want to be beautiful," says Phyllis with glee. Phyllis is enjoying the fact that her cocky landlady, my mother, has lost all control of the situation. I can tell that she is looking forward to rehashing this debacle with Betty over endless glasses of homemade turnip wine.

After each application, Irene places an untouched jar or tin of that particular product on the occasional table. Clearly she is hoping for a big sale. Betty lights a cigarette to steady her nerves. Smoke wreaths both client and professional. Irene, in the full flood of her creativity, seems unfazed by this. She is smoke resistant.

Irene rummages in her bag of tricks.

"You must change your eyelids, my dear," she says, extricating an eye shadow from her stock, holding it aloft, and declaiming, "Thees is your color."

Nobody can accuse Irene of being tentative or perfunctory. Eye shadow in one hand, applicator in the other, she is attacking Betty's upper lids as if her life depended on it.

"We must not be stingy with ourselves," she says, as she reaches for the pot of color time and time again, adding, "You will buy six of these, which is lasting you ze rest of zuh month."

"We'll see . . ." croaks Betty, in a halfhearted attempt to reassert herself.

"Ha! Perfect!" says Irene with a self-satisfied air. She stands on tiptoes, leans back, and admires the whole effect. My sister and I stand up and ready ourselves for the formal unveiling.

"Not yet!" barks Irene, causing us both to flinch. We are not used to being yelled at. Our parents rarely have occasion to discipline us. Betty controls our behavior through her own brand of snobbery. Her technique is quite clever. She established early on in our lives that there were only two types of people in the world. We were free to join either group.

There were the losers who pick their noses, hurl abuse at passers-by, and tread dog poo into the house. These individuals, according to Betty, "have no bloody savoir faire." These people will spend their lives eating greasy fish and chips and working in factories. They contribute nothing to the world: "They take in oxygen and give out carbon dioxide."

And then there are the fabulous people, the life enhancers, people who, even if they work in the same factories, always somehow manage to look great, smell great, and never arrive at other people's houses empty-handed. These are the people who are eating ham festooned with pineapple chunks. These people are committed to the concept of *gracious living*. These are *our people*.

Betty Doonan, city of contrasts. Despite her rough background and lack of education, Betty is a self-invented glamorous eccentric with an unconventional worldview. While she loves skewering the pomposity and conventionality of the English middle class, she is also committed to grabbing her share of the pineapple chunks and leaving the peat bogs behind.

Irene takes out a large and quite theatrical powder puff. She douses it in ivory face powder and whaps Betty's face repeatedly.

"This will fix the makeups and stops it sliding!"

Irene removes the pink plastic cape with a flourish, à la toreador.

Finally Betty stands up. She turns to face us, and we both gasp. Even Phyllis gasps. Betty looks in the mirror and winces.

She does not look beautiful. She looks nothing Liz Taylor. In truth, she does not look human at all. Betty looks like an earthenware garden gnome that has been hosed with Technicolor concrete and then sifted with flour.

And those eyelids. That color!

My mum hates tyrants and imperialists and mean drunks. She loathes nasty women who poach other women's husbands and she dislikes snooty women who assume she is common because she wears seamed stockings and is generally more glamorous than the other ladies who ride the bus. And she definitely hates anyone who does not respect the interests of her people, the people of Northern Ireland.

But there is something she hates far more than any of the above: blue eye shadow.

Blue eye shadow is her bête noire.

Blue eye shadow is unforgivable. Blue eye shadow is contemptible and pathetic.

If you had listened to Betty Doonan, you would have thought the wearing of powder blue eye shadow signified the end of civilization.

For Betty, eye makeup is quite simple: a metallic gray smoky eyelid, accentuated with a discreet application of mascara, made liquid by the introduction to her cake of kohl by a small quantity of her own spit. A smidgen of gray eye shadow, yes, but not blue. *Never* blue!

She has made her feelings on the subject known to everyone in our household at one time or another.

According to my Betty, blue eye shadow is worn by two very different but equally disappointing groups of women.

First group: the genteel frumps. These poor, unfortunate, unassuming ladies hope, with their softly powdered lids, to recall the innocence of cornflowers, the poetry of bluebells, and the sincerity of forget-me-nots. These are the kind of women who serve little cakes on doilies. They are twee.

Group two: the rough trouts. The old boilers. The tarts. These predatory harlots wear lashings of wet-looking blue eye shadow in a vain attempt to camouflage their sin and assume some of the floral innocence of group one.

I fully expect Betty to fly across the room and strangle Irene with her bare hands.

She stares at her shimmering blue lids, unable to speak.

How thin her lips are! Without that Joan Crawford bow, Betty looks as if she has forgotten to pop in her top teeth.

But the real horror is the maquillage itself. There is no way to describe how grotesque that blue looks against the orange pancake, the rouge, and the pale pink lipstick. This dissonant color combination—orange, red, pink, and blue—seems more appropriate for one of Betty's culinary triumphs. As part of her cooking-with-color regime, Betty sometimes alternates sliced tomatoes with tinned peach halves. Instead of transforming my mother into Liz Taylor, Irene has transformed my mother into a Saturday night supper.

Betty has, for the first time in my short life, actually broken a sweat. I can see a moist patch growing under her arm. This is very unusual. Betty never sweats. (She uses a foolproof product called Odorono—as in, "odor? oh no!"—a product so strong that, even after riding her white bicycle up the steep hill to our house, she never shows any sign of perspiration.)

Before you can say Liz Taylor Hilton Fisher Burton, Irene begins her sales pitch. Having dragged herself up our hill and then spent the last hour transforming my mother into a vision of hideousness, she now feels entirely justified in strong-arming Betty into buying as much product as possible.

Irene totals up the cost of all the products, which Betty is under no obligation to buy but which she would be out of her mind not to.

Betty is standing speechless in front of the mirror.

The pushy Irene prattles on.

"Do you have any makeup removal pads?" says Betty, interrupting Irene midspiel.

"If you buy all zis makeups I give you ze pads for free," says Irene, her accent worsening now that her sales pitch is reaching that make-or-break point.

"I only want the pads."

Irene glares at Betty. Anger twitches across her face. This emotion is closely followed by sadness. The unfolding scenario is obviously familiar to Irene. She ding-dongs her way into a given house, disfigures the occupant with her heavy-handed cosmetics application, and is then rejected.

"Please buy a lipstick!" begs the world's worst Avon lady.

"Lemme think about it," says Betty and ushers her through the hallway toward the front door.

As she is helping Irene into her plastic raincoat, Narg bursts out of the room where she eats and sleeps and listens to the radio for hours with mad Uncle Ken.

Narg is Betty's nemesis, her deranged and belligerent mother-in-law. My sister and I gave her the name Narg because it was Gran backwards and because it was shorter that Genghis Khan.

Narg focuses on Betty's face.

"Oh! You look loverly today!" she says without a trace of hostility and irony.

This is the last straw.

"I left a cigarette burning!" Betty abandons Irene and bolts in the direction of the kitchen.

My sister and I watch as Irene trudges off down the path. She pauses just at the place where the gypsy spits. She turns and waves.

"I come in month viz ze new makeups."

Betty cannot hear her. Betty is already hanging over the sink, scrubbing furiously to erase the curse of the Avon lady.

As I look back at that fateful afternoon, I feel vaguely homicidal toward that Avon lady.

The thickset lady from Krakow was able to sow seeds of doubt where none had previously existed. She mined Betty's psyche and found a horrid truffle of low self-esteem and self-doubt. She then proceeded to dig it up and grate it all over Betty.

Somehow this unlikely character managed to touch a nerve of insecurity Betty Doonan, my mother, the toughest, most stylish broad in Reading, the only woman I ever saw wear gold-flecked rubber galoshes over her spike-heeled shoes.

Betty's vintage glamour was timeless and fabulous and it suited her. It was singular and it had an eccentric vintage appeal. Twenty years out of date, but so what? Betty had a retro-chic look that she had honed over decades until it fit her like a glove. Only when it was obliterated did we come to realize the full extent of its pure majesty.

As you set off on your journey toward glamorous eccentricity, you must be on your guard for charlatans and lunatics. Theirs is an age-old technique deployed by "beauty experts" the world over. First marinate your victim with a bunch of vaguely insulting observations. Then, when the flesh has softened a bit, dive in for the kill with all fangs bared.

You have been warned.

*"Being corseted down to seventeen inches
in a flowing black silk riding habit and
sitting sidesaddle and jumping horses
shows a real dedication to glamour, no?"*

DITA VON TEESE

*The stylish queen of contemporary burlesque
and artistic striptease responds to the Eccentric
Glamour questionnaire.*

What are you wearing?

Vintage 1940s lounging pajamas in magenta satin, *chinoise* style
with very wide legs. When I'm relaxing at home, I love pajamas
and robes . . . but the glamorous variety only, no plaid fleece,
and no sweatpants!

**When did you first realize that you might in fact be a
glamorous eccentric?**

When I was in first grade and I was angry that I wasn't allowed
to wear my fancy special occasion dress to school. I couldn't
understand why I couldn't wear something frilly and feminine
and pretty every day! I began to plot my womanhood . . . I
promised myself I would dress like the femmes fatales I saw in
the old movies my mother and I watched together. I also used
to steal my mother's lingerie to try on. I became somewhat

obsessed with lingerie. To me, it was and still is a symbol of womanhood and femininity.

Were your parents horrified?

When I was a teenager, they might have thought I was a little crazy for going out dressed the way I did—vintage hats and dresses paired with corsets mostly. Sometimes I would even dress in man drag Dietrich style. When I was eighteen, I remember being inspired by an erotic novel by Anaïs Nin and I wanted to dress like a lesbian in 1930s Paris, so I found a vintage tuxedo, combed my hair into marcel waves, and trotted out the door, Bakelite cigar holder hanging from my burgundy lips. They were probably more amused by me than anything, not horrified.

Are you prone to mood swings?

I'm not a very moody person; I'm generally quite agreeable and pleasant. The only time I'm really hard to be around is when I'm stripped of my glamour!

Have you ever been mocked for any of your glamorous eccentricities?

Sure, all the time! I *live* for being considered unusual! The kiss of death with regard to style and chic is to "follow" fashion, or to try to fit in with the norm.

What is the most eccentrically glam thing in your closet?

Perhaps one of the many pairs of shoes I have that are impossible to walk in. And when I say impossible, I mean it. We're not talking about six-inch heels, we're talking about shoes that are literally meant to be crawled in! And I suppose some of my tightest corsets might be considered eccentric or shocking by some people.

Have you ever wished you could trade in your life of glamorous eccentricity for one of dreary conformity?
Never! Not even for one second. Dressing for glamour is what I've dreamed of since I was a little girl. It's something that is deep within me, a true love of glamour and what it can do for any woman if she wants it!

When does eccentric glamour become idiocy?
I don't think it really does. Even when I see someone whose style I don't care for, I still appreciate that she is wearing what she likes regardless of what anyone thinks. There is always some idiot calling some other person an idiot, isn't there?

Who is your inspirational icon of glamorous eccentricity?
The Marchesa Casati. I would like to give every person who thinks she is *so* risqué and so eccentric a book called *Infinite Variety* so she can read about what eccentricity *really* is and who was living it in a big way almost a hundred years ago! "I want to be a living work of art!" the Marchesa said.

I also love Empress Elizabeth of Austria, who seemed pretty eccentric to me too. Being corseted down to seventeen inches in a flowing black silk riding habit and sitting sidesaddle and jumping horses shows a real dedication to glamour, no?

Do men think you are hot?
Some of them do, but you know, I wouldn't dare generalize. Everyone has a different idea of what is sexy, and I can appreciate and respect that. And I care more about winning over the women and inspiring them to dress up and embrace glamour than I do about making men think I'm hot. I'm a girls' girl—I think that the men aren't enough of a challenge!

What is the thing that most offends your glamorously eccentric sensibilities?

When a magazine or photographer wants to photograph me with no makeup on, or in casual clothes. I think about women like Marlene Dietrich and Marilyn Monroe. They were never stripped of their glamour. They *knew* better. They knew what glamour means, and it's about the allure and enchantment of mystery.

Where do you wish to be buried, and in what?

Père-Lachaise cemetery in Paris. I wouldn't want to be buried in anything *too* special—I would want to make sure my favorite pieces live on and are enjoyed by someone else! But perhaps it would be the ideal time for my most extreme corset and a pair of those unwalkable heels I was talking about . . .

CHAPTER 3

What the Hookers
Are Wearing

The meaning of snakeskin culottes

Tyra Banks looks like a gorgeous marmalade cat. I swear I can actually hear her purring. Though her cleavage-baring showbiz glamour is fairly standard, she manages to inject a dash of glamorous eccentricity into her look by constantly changing her wigs, weaves, and maquillage, often with a feline theme. The result is quite intimidating. It gives me an odd feeling. She is so extraordinarily and voluptuously catlike that, standing next to her, I feel as if I've turned into a mouse or a gerbil or possibly Linda Hunt.

Nonetheless, I am quite happy. Excited, even. My heart is beating. The cameras are set to roll. It's 2004 and I am about to make my reality television debut.

I am in the running to become America's Next Top Model! Almost. I am what they call "a guest presenter."

Tyra outlines my assignment in the crisply articulated tones that have become the signature of this riveting show: My task is to teach the contestants how to dress for a "go-see"—how these young model aspirants should present themselves when auditioning for bookings.

As soon as the girls enter the studio, I am instructed to commence the shenanigans by offering a gloves-off critique of their personal style. The contestants have been told—via Tyra-mail—to dress to express.

Action! The dozen or so hopefuls troop into view.

I am at a loss for words, but not for long.

"So you ladies are dressed for a go-see, correct?"

Collective nod.

"Precisely who are you going to see?" I continue. "I hope it's not Anna Wintour. I have a horrible feeling it might be Larry Flynt."

Silence. They are clearly unaware of the existence of either *Vogue* or *Hustler* or their respective editors in chief.

I realize that I am going to have to be a little more direct.

"Why are you all dressed like a bunch of strippers?" I query, in a supportive and caring sort of way, adding, "There's a difference between porno and fashion, don't ya know!"

The gals tug at their tube tops and try in vain to hoist their Juicy Couture velours up over their various areas. Clearly they have succumbed to the pressures of porno-chic. They have been unable to "say no to ho!"

Their heads remain unbowed. They stare defiantly at me.

To better make my point, I single out a young lady called Catie for special consideration. Catie is wearing—I use the word loosely—a skimpy halter top and a crotch-length denim skirt. On her feet are black patent porno pumps with six-inch heels. The pièce de résistance? Black leg warmers with stirrups. They hook under the insteps of her shoes and rise to within about two inches of Catie's skirt hem. Suffice it to say, the overall look is not Jackie Kennedy.

"What words would you use to best describe your outfit?" I ask, in a halfhearted attempt to be inclusive and interactive.

Catie shrugs.

"You need to go down to the docks, see what all the hookers are wearing and avoid it," I advise, eliciting guffaws and frantic thumbs-ups from the tension-mongering producers.

A large tear rolls down Catie's cheek. The camera zooms in for the kill.

(At the time I felt horrible and suspected that I might have participated in the culture of bullying that drives trash TV. Later my guilt subsided when an assistant producer informed me that Catie is the chief cryer of the series. As my old Irish granddad used to say, "Her bladder is awful near her eyeballs.")

"Catie, why are you crying?" I ask.

"Because you just [sob] called me a ho [sob] on national television."

At that very moment, thanks to good old Catie, I have a startling insight. Catie's tears, I realize, are profoundly significant. They reveal a shocking truth about these poor ingénues.

These gals do not understand that clothes have *meaning*.

They were told to "dress to express," and that is what they did, randomly and without any sense that they might have the option to express something other than slutty availability or a general commitment to the porn industry.

I feel bad for them. They are ill equipped to survive in the big city because they simply do not understand the significance of any of their fashion choices. Unless I intervene, these gals are all doomed to go through life dressed like a bunch of third-rate hoochie dancers, all the while thinking that they look perfectly normal and respectable.

Maybe I can be the one to open their eyes. I decide to give it a shot.

"Girls! Girls! Listen to me," I command, in a stern Miss Jean Brodie voice. "I did not say that Catie *is* a ho. I said that she is dressed like one."

Blank expressions.

"Don't you see, your clothing, what you choose to wear every day, it speaks volumes about you. It is a form of nonverbal communication! You have to make sure that your clothing is in sync with who you are."

From the puzzled looks on the faces of these attention junkies, I realize that this is a notion that has never ever ever occurred to them before. They are marching through the world, shopping, shopping, shopping, impulsively wearing all kinds of freaky ensembles, and never once have they stopped to think that fashion might be playing such a powerful role in all of our lives.

I continue: "What you wear says everything about who you are. Long before you open your mouth, people are drawing conclusions about you based on your appearance. If you dress like a stripper, Catie, people will assume that you *are* a stripper, which is okay only if you are in fact a stripper."

"What about *your* outfit?" says a fiery little troublemaker called Jenascia.

Suddenly I feel rather self-conscious. All eyes are on me. Nervously, I take inventory of my ensemble: a gaudy Paul Smith floral print shirt, skinny Prada pants, a Gucci belt, and suede Dolce & Gabbana Beatle boots. On my pinkie is a boulder-sized gold Dior ring. I realize, with a surge of relief, that my clothing choices are completely and utterly in sync with *moi*! One glance at me, even from across the street, and you can tell exactly what you are dealing with: a label-crazed gay bloke—mutton dressed as lamb—who understands the utter pointlessness of growing old gracefully and still thinks he is living in mod London circa 1966.

"We're not here to talk about me," I say, just as the director yells, "Cut!"

We're done. I throw on my knee-length belted Rudolph Nureyev 1960s Burberry trench and sweep out of the studio, safe in the knowledge that Tyra's gals still have no idea what the hell I am talking about.

In fairness to my semiclad chums on *America's Next Top Model*, they are not the only perpetrators of this particular crime. All over America, people are making kamikaze choices about what to wear. They are misrepresenting the goods. They are letting their clothes write checks that their personalities cannot cash.

What about you?

Are you a nun in showgirl's clothing? Are your outfits telegraphing misinformation about your personality?

Breaking the Code

To better illustrate my point, permit me to expound on the meaning and significance of some fashion basics.

Let's start with an easy one: the color red.

Red plays a key role in the development of eccentric glamour. Red is the catalyst that can take you—Gypsy, Existentialist, or Socialite—from dull spectator to star attraction, but only if you use her wisely. (Colors, like ships, are female.)

Red is wild. She is unsettling. She intrigues. Wear red and other women will assume that you are a predatory vixen who is out to steal their husbands and suck the blood of their children. If you think I'm exaggerating, please remember that it's the red Lexus that always gets the speeding ticket. Wear red and people will take notice.

The color red is synonymous with everything racy and outrageous. Before you buy that gorgeous red velvet cocktail frock, keep in mind the following: Red is the color of wicked divorcées and Chinese opium dens.

However, if you wear her right—harness that crazy bitch!—the color red has genuine allure.

Having inveighed against the slutty styles du jour, I would like to take a moment to clarify the difference between looking cheap and horrible—see the Evas of Chapter 1—and looking alluring.

Allure is timeless. Allure is smoldering beauty and sensuality, as opposed to overt pastie-twirling sexual availability. Allure is that irresistible, mysterious charm which never fails to mesmerize the viewer, regardless of gender. Allure is about crossing your legs, as opposed to spreading them as you clamber out of that Lexus, sans panties.

The clothing of Azzedine Alaia has genuine allure. Allure is Jeanne Moreau. Allure is Cyd Charisse. (Excuse the old school examples, but, in the age of Britney and Lindsay, allure has fallen by the wayside.) Red can give you an eccentric and stylish allure without the sleaze.

A beautifully cut red bustier dress will convey the idea that you are unpredictable, crazy, and louche but not in a tawdry Paris Hilton kind of way.

Test the waters with a pair of blood red, over-the-top, strappy high-heeled shoes. Team them with a simple "secretarial" skirt and blouse, pick up your purse, and hit the streets. Brace yourself: Remember what the ruby slippers did for Dorothy and don't blame me if you end up at four in the morning doing the tango with a distinguished older gentleman who is graying at the temples and wants to whisk you off to Argentina.

Apply extreme caution when wearing red in the workplace. Even a simple demure red outfit—a cashmere twinset—can turn you into the office lightning rod. If you are crafty, you can use this to your advantage. To gain the upper hand in an upcoming negotiation, try wearing a flaming red silk blouse and painting your nails red.

Warning: Scientists have shown that the color red causes a rise in blood pressure. Don't wear your scalpel-cut red frock around people in fragile health: You might kill someone. Which brings us to black and the wearing thereof.

Black is a great deal more complex than red. Saint, academic, devil, or punk, black has so many dissonant connotations, all of them extreme. The associations run the gamut from Maria von Trapp to Sid Vicious and back again.

First and foremost, the wearing of black will give you an edge, hence its popularity with rebels and reprobates.

Rockers have always worn black to suggest that they might be in league with the devil. This, for some strange reason, is seen as a positive thing. In this particular milieu, black imbues the wearer with instant hip and alternative cred. Look at it this way, if Ozzy Osbourne had worn a pink jumpsuit when he bit the head off that bat, people would probably have laughed and mistaken him for Rip Taylor.

Existentialists take note: Black can start a revolution. The wearing of black will add to the drama of your transformative odyssey. For maximum effect, choose from the following: a black leather James Dean jacket; a pair of black toreador pants; a black jersey Martha Graham dress with a terrifyingly huge circular skirt, or how about a pair of black crocodile thigh boots with tassels on the zippers?

But what if you desire to minimize the chaos in your life?

Glamorous eccentrics with children, lodgers, or unruly pets may well be looking to restore order rather than create disorder. If you wish to intimidate or subdue those around you, black clothing—especially anything with epaulets—is your best friend. The fascists of the last century—in England they were called the Blackshirts—wore black to intimidate the unruly masses. It may well do the same for you. Caution: If you find yourself jackbooting through the living room in order to get the kids to do their homework, this is an indication that you may have gone too far.

Whether you are a Gypsy, an Existentialist, or a Socialite, black is profoundly practical. A black coat is probably about the most useful garment you can own. It doesn't show the dirt and instantly covers up a hastily assembled less interesting outfit, allowing you to project eccentric glamour with the minimum of effort.

Keep a diverse selection of black coats in your hall closet. As you leave the house, you can select the one that best fits the role you wish to play.

Want to look pious? Try an itchy wool puritan coat.

If you are feeling more like a hired assassin or a spy, belt yourself into a classic trench.

A black, tiered highwayman cape will make you look romantic and swashbuckling. (Not recommended for munchkins under five feet.)

Before we move from black to white, here's a hot tip for dumb blonds who are interviewing for a job in the field of nuclear physics or, for that matter, in the field of anything. As previously stated in Chapter 1, black is great for making you appear more intelligent and thoughtful than you are. Throw on a black turtleneck and your IQ mysteriously appears to rise.

This is not the case with white. White speaks more to money than intelligence.

White suggests that you are fabulously wealthy and do not work for a living. Just as people wear black to hide grime and stains, people wear white to demonstrate to the world that they are very, very, very unconcerned about sky-high dry-cleaning bills. Wearing a white Chanel suit says, "I am a very wealthy woman who has never scrubbed out a toilet and, God willing, never will." Rappers, both male and female, love to wear white: it shows off their diamond jewelry and suggests that the wearer may have transcended the grime of the ghetto and has no intention of returning.

A caution to white folks who wear white: White shoes and bags, while perfectly lovely on an Afro-Socialite such as Alicia Keys, invariably transform a Caucasian female into a nurse. If the white lady in question is bejeweled and Chaneled she runs the risk of being mistaken not just for a regular nurse, but for an extremely wealthy nurse.

Regarding the nurse curse: Back in the '60s, white was a huge part of the French futurist movement (think Courrèges and Cardin). A stiff white piqué micromini A-line dress—worn with white go-go boots—was the grooviest, most insanely fabulous thing a gal could own . . . for a microsecond. I once asked Emanuel Ungaro—a disciple of Courrèges and a playa in this scene during his youth—why the '60s futurist explosion was so short-lived. *"C'est un peu orthopédique, non?"* was his revealing reply.

Though white can be problematique for eccentrically glamorous females, the same is not true for the male. Think of John Travolta in that fabulous white suit in *Saturday Night Fever*!

I have a pal called Igor—a Russian—who wears nothing but white. He is tall and straight (!) and handsome. A recreational nudist and yoga devotee, aristocratic Igor is an uninhibited, glamorously eccentric bloke who does not have the macho inhibitions of the typical American dude. In a sea of conformity, he is a beacon of individuality. His handsome idiosyncratic bearing makes him irresistible to both men and women.

I am very jealous of Igor. We short males do not have the same carte blanche. When a little guy like me wears a white suit, it's only a matter of time before somebody starts shouting, "Ze plane! Ze Plane!"

Breaking the Code cont. . . .

One of the most vaunted trends of recent years has been the "volume" trend: big skirts! Billowing capes! All hail the queen! Her Majesty is coming through!

What do these larger-than-life garments signify to the on-looker?

A wide Prada or vintage dirndl skirt screams, "I am impor-tant. I am Marie Antoinette." A capacious taffeta cocoon yells, "I own everything in sight! Get the hell out of the way!" In-timidatingly voluminous clothes suggest that you are deposed royalty, or at least an insane person who believes he or she is deposed royalty.

Wearing a big wide skirt can have a practical application. It is highly recommended for people who are in a hurry and live in crowded towns with narrow streets. You become, courtesy of your garments, a human snowplow.

At the other end of the scale we have infantile clothing: tiny childlike items, Mary Janes teamed with scaled-up versions of dolly dresses and rompers. This sends one message and one message only: It suggests in no uncertain terms that the wearer is resistant to the demands of adult life. Think Courtney Love circa 1998.

For an adult to be thought of as infantile is not a good thing: People will attribute the worst aspects of childhood to you. They will assume that you are prone to petulance and various other idiocies, including foot stamping and drooling. Think early Courtney Love again.

The adoption of eccentric glamour requires that you demonstrate a certain adult competence. Please do not buy clothes at OshKosh, even if you can fit into them. Yes, I know that Edie Sedgwick, Warhol's eternal style icon, wowed the fashion pundits of her day with her innovative microkilts—purchased from kiddies' school uniform shops—but look what happened to her.

Though infantile dressing is provocative and unsettling, it cannot compare with the wearing of animal skins. When you don the pelt of a particular animal—snake, beaver, marmoset—the effect on the viewer is dramatic or, as Flavor Flav always said on his reality show *Flavor of Love*, "dramatical." You will instantly and shockingly be perceived as having the same traits as your chosen varmint. Dramatical, *non*?

The wearing of moleskin says, "I am soft and velvety and mysterious and like to hide underground."

A mink coat says, "I'm a tough cookie. Though I may not have the wherewithal to actually kill you, please expect to be nipped on a regular basis."

The pelts of predators always give the impression that you are a man-stealing, window-smashing home wrecker. This also applies to animal-printed fabric. The message of a leopard-print jumpsuit is clear, "I am a huntress who delights in eating the offal of her prey."

Fox tails create the impression that you are wily. Lambskin connotes innocence. The exception is Persian lamb or Astrakhan: The wearing of this particular pelt says, "I am a cruel bitch who does not care that I am wearing the skin of an unborn animal." The one common denominator? Fur always conveys the idea that you are rrrrrrrich!

Snake goes farther: The wearing of snakeskin not only suggests wealth, it gives you an air of venomous mystery. The biblical connotations of the snake—combined with the prevalence of snake phobia—make it an unwise choice for religious occasions such as weddings and christenings. The sight of you quaffing champagne and wiggling about in a snake-print cocktail sheath will prove very distracting to the average priest or rabbi.

A Devilishly Provocative Red Thong

As now must surely be crystal clear, your wardrobe choices constitute a clear and explicit form of nonverbal communication. People will make all kinds of assumptions, grotesque and otherwise, about who you are based on what you wear. They can and will judge a book by its cover.

There are only two things you can do with this information: You can use it either to conceal or to reveal. To obfuscate or to communicate. To camouflage or to walk boldly into the spotlight, that is the question.

Though I am a staunch advocate of the latter, there are occasions where disguise is permissible.

If you have a sleazy criminal past and are eager to make a fresh start, you must make every effort to inject a little wholesome innocence into your attire. Like Blanche DuBois in *A Streetcar Named Desire*, you can drape yourself in floating chiffons and "summer furs" to obscure the sordid, desperate, fugitive you.

Like Anjelica Huston's character in *The Grifters*, you can wear a pristine white mother-of-the-bride suit to hide the blackness of your heart.

Like Monica Lewinsky, you can dress like a varsity ingénue, all the while entertaining crazed erotic fantasies about the commander in chief, for whose delectation you have secretly donned a devilishly provocative red thong.

Misrepresenting yourself through your clothing is also justified if your survival is at stake. If you are trying to elude the attentions of an unwanted sociopathic suitor, you may opt to disfigure yourself with an oversize Coogi sweater and a bubble wig. It may even behoove you to leave your legs unshaved. Think Amy Sedaris in *Strangers with Candy*.

If the suitor in question is particularly persistent, you may find it necessary to make yourself even more repellant: Stick-on boils and warts can be purchased at most finer novelty/joke shops.

I hope life has not catapulted you on the kind of trajectory where you feel it necessary to deploy this kind of duplicity.

I hope you can take the path of righteousness and tell it like it is.

I hope you can reveal all and use your appearance to express the glamorous, eccentric, God-given, and essential you.

Before you make any purchase—big or small—take a moment to consider the meaning and significance of what you are buying. Keep in mind that each and every blouse and pocketbook has the potential to communicate something horribly fatal or utterly fabulous about you.

If you get confused and frustrated, simply take a walk down to the docks, fill your lungs with fresh salty air, and take a long, hard look at what the hookers are wearing.

*"I love the simplicity of
the Muslim white wrap for burial,
especially after my colorful life."*

IMAN

The first black supermodel, philanthropist, entre-
preneur, the stuff of fashion legend, married to a
man who spent many years wearing a feather boa—
the greatest glamorous eccentric male of all time,
Mr. David Bowie—responds to the Eccentric Glamour
questionnaire.

What are you wearing?
My at-home uniform: a red cashmere Halston caftan.

When did you first realize that you might in fact be a glamorous eccentric?
At the age of twelve when I looked for a Missoni print in Cairo . . . which I did find and paired it with white tights and large Jackie O. white sunglasses.

Were your parents horrified?
Of course, but that was the point!

Are you prone to mood swings?
Isn't everyone? I am very suspicious of people who aren't.

Have you ever been mocked for any of your glamorous eccentricities?
I can't remember! But as Oscar Wilde said: "To love oneself is the beginning of a life-long romance."

What is the most eccentrically glam thing in your closet?
A long, backless patchwork suede dress—very Cleopatra Jones.

Have you ever wished you could trade in your life of glamorous eccentricity for one of dreary conformity?
God, NO! How boring. I leave that to all those poor starlets who hire "stylists." We are a vanishing tribe; nevertheless, we are much needed.

When does eccentric glamour become idiocy?
When you pay attention to what other people think, or when you pare it down. I say *commit*!

Who is your inspirational icon of glamorous eccentricity?
Verushka now and, of course, always Isabella Blow.

Do men think you are hot?
I know they do—especially the ones with great taste.

What is the thing that most offends your glamorously eccentric sensibilities?
When the tabloid fashion police don't get it and allocate you to "when bad clothes happen to good people."

Where do you wish to be buried, and in what?
I would like to be cremated and my ashes scattered from the highest point in Bali . . . but being a Muslim, it might not happen. I love the simplicity of the Muslim white wrap for burial, especially after my colorful life.

CHAPTER 4

Freud's Handbag

Nobody wants an old clutch

Eccentric glamour is about *not* toeing the line. It's about taking a walk on the wild side. It's about swimming against the tide.

As a card-carrying glamorous eccentric, you must find new and original ways to break free from the herd.

If everyone is going blond, dye your hair dark brown, or let it go gray.

If the magazines tout thigh boots, buy ankle boots, and if you cannot find ankle boots, buy thigh boots and cut them off.

If sushi is hot, eat offal.

If orange becomes the new chartreuse, then start wearing cerise.

Keep moving the goalposts. Be utterly relentless.

Busting a new taboo may be far easier than you think. There's no need to look far. For example, there could be a great opportunity lurking on the top shelf of your closet. I'm talking about that beaten-up Prada doctor's bag circa 1998.

Dust it off, dangle it from the crook of your arm, and brace yourself for the reaction. Why? Because, believe it or not, the most transgressive, insanely provocative, shocking, attention-getting eccentrically glamorous thing any gal in the world could do right now, at this exact point in history, is to appear in public sporting an *old bag*.

Yes, a beaten-up, out-of-date purse!

Using the "c" word, on-the-job boozing, hairy pits, public sex, hideous halitosis, unmanicured extremities, removing a chafing bra on the bus—none of these no-nos will come close to causing the frisson of fascination that will be occasioned by the parading in public of a déjà vu, has-been, ungroovy purse.

The mania for spanking-new purses is a comparatively recent phenomenon. In days of yore, ladies were happy to tote an old bag, the life of which they prolonged with occasional oilings and restitchings. When the lining wore out, it was replaced. When the clasp fell off, a new one was installed.

Not so today.

Handbag refreshment has, in the first decade of this new millennium, reached some kind of sick, frenzied crescendo. Based on purse sales at Barneys, not to mention the West African street vendor who flogs knockoffs around the corner from my house, the average female is now buying a new purse every fifteen minutes.

What on earth are the ladies doing with their unwanted wrinkly old bags? At this point in time, I would have expected to see massive slag heaps of discarded Kate Spades, Lanvins, Coaches, and Balenciagas accumulating outside every apartment building in every city in the entire universe. You sneaky purseaholics! Are you eating them? Are you cutting them into strips and blending them in the Cuisinart?

Regardless of where they are storing or secreting them, and regardless of whether it's a one-off velour Louis Vuitton number that you had to wait two years for, or some squishy vinyl clutch from Kmart, this demented compulsion to buy handbag after handbag suggests the presence of a new and horrid pandemic: These ladies are clearly suffering from hysterical accessory gathering syndrome, HAGS for short.

Does this compulsion have sinister psychological underpinnings? Don't be silly. Of course it does.

According to Sigmund Freud, handbags are vaginal symbols.

It's important not to take this notion too literally. If you dream that you are frantically searching for your purse, it does not necessarily mean that you have mislaid your vagina.

If you are a guy and you dream that your mother is stuffing you into her Fendi baguette, you may want to stop doing her hair or giving her facials or whatever it is that you are doing that is producing these horrid nightmares.

If you have a recurring dream that the strap keeps breaking on your purse, don't get too analytical: It could simply mean that you recently bought a really cheap purse and you are harboring a deep unconscious insecurity about the quality thereof.

Once you accept the hypothesis that vaginas and handbags are 100 percent synonymous, the world becomes a very interesting place.

Look at that Socialite over there with her buckled and padlocked Chloe Paddington bag: Is she transmitting a message of chastity or of bondage?

Look at the teeth on that Existentialist Prada zippered number! Vagina dentata, anyone?

And that Gypsy with the Coach patchwork bucket shoulder tote, what subconscious motivations are causing her to fiddle so obsessively with her suede fringe?

What of the celebs? Are they suffering from HAGS too? There is a tradition among red-carpet strutters to pose bagless before their adoring public. When Somalian supermodel Iman—a titan in the world of eccentric glamour—appears at an opening, she is always, fascinatingly and enigmatically, sans handbag. When I challenged her about her motivation a few years back, she was typically defiant and regal: "I think it's so much more glamorous to be purseless. I already have the perfect accessories—my husband David Bowie and his bodyguard!" Who is carrying Iman's nude lip gloss? Why, the bodyguard, of course.

Fortunately for retailers, most women are not in a position to inoculate themselves against the HAGS epidemic with a lip-gloss-toting bodyguard. *Au contraire*, many gals are carrying several purses at once, suggesting a terrifying hydra of multiple pudenda.

One such person is author and former *Vogue* cover girl Louise de Teliga. When touring to promote her novel *Fashion Slaves*, Louise typically arrived at book signings carrying a pink Prada tote. Inside this capacious fleshy receptacle lurks a teensy brown grosgrain Anya Hindmarch number with a bow and two adorably furry brown mink pompoms.

I asked her if balls might indicate a latent castration impulse. "Quite possibly," said the former cover girl with a laugh, "At the very least, I'm stashing a small brown vagina, with balls, inside a big pink vagina . . ."

Eccentric glamour involves bucking the trends and, regardless of whether you are a Gypsy, an Existentialist, or a Socialite, it means developing a strong, confident contrarian point of view.

With that in mind, I strongly advise you to step off your Freudian whirligig of handbag refreshment.

Do it now.

Allow yourself one handbag and one handbag only. Pour all your money into one striking-but-timeless receptacle—one that best reflects your persona—and carry it always.

Socialites can snag the Hermès Birkin they have always dreamed of.

Existentialists should carry something improbable: a Japanese school satchel, a provocatively conservative black patent vintage Margaret Thatcher handbag, or a defunct airline bag. If you are an Existentialist/Socialite, buy a white Birkin and personalize it with Magic Marker.

A Gypsy gal should cart everything around in a capaciously scrotal velour sac of her own making.

The key is never to change: Carry this bag morning, noon, and night.

Allowing yourself to become synonymous with an accessory can make you more memorable and relieves you of the burden of transference. No, not Freudian transference: I'm talking about transferring all your crap from one bag to another every time you switch.

What, you may well ask, should you do with all those previous, perniciously pricey Prada purses?

Girls! Let's take those old bags and put them to good use! Meet me down by South Street Seaport. We will throw all your unwanted Louis Vuittons and Coaches into the water and create a fab new landfill.

We can call it HAG Island.

"I once wore a pair of jeans and sneakers on the subway and never did that again because of how approachable and vulnerable that suddenly made me. A dash of eccentric glamour gives you the power to keep the wrong kind of men away."

ISABEL TOLEDO

*Fashion designer, Surrealist, realist, proud Cubana,
and wife of Ruben Toledo responds to the Eccentric
Glamour questionnaire.*

What are you wearing?

I am wearing a pair of boxer shorts called Fellini and a fine
Swiss silk rib camisole, old beat-up surfer flip-flops, and a huge
black organdy crinoline that I whipped together last night.

**When did you first realize that you might in fact be a
glamorous eccentric?**

In my early teens I started to make my own clothes and put
them together with my sisters' hand-me-downs that I would
reconfigure to fit my too-skinny frame. Plaid pants would
become a skirt, corduroy minis over jeans, layered shorts,
anything to appear a bit "thicker." Dancing was a big part
of my Cuban immigrant social life. People would wait to see
what I had cooked up for my weekend dance hall appearance,
a charmeuse wrap dress, Chinese pajamas with high heels—all

this at the age of twelve or thirteen. This is what gave me the confidence to speak through clothes.

Were your parents horrified?
Mom was horrified indeed—she of the matching pocketbook and shoes—because my sisters always tried hard to look conventionally attractive. She insisted I was being difficult. My father was amused as he sat in his very proper recliner waiting for me to appear from my room for a night out.

Are you prone to mood swings?
Clothing mood swings? Absolutely! I still wear clothes I had in high school, so I do believe in continuity and finding old friends in the closet, but I enjoy changing my clothes as often as possible during the day. With me it can be formal in the morning, militant at midday, nostalgia in late afternoon, and a uniform for night.

Have you ever been mocked for any of your glamorous eccentricities?
I live by this Oscar Wilde quotation: "When critics disagree, the artist is in accord with himself."

What is the most eccentrically glam thing in your closet?
Eccentricity doesn't hang in my closet; it sits around the house. My collection of galoshes lives in the garden as a sculpture when not worn. A Portuguese widow's shawl lies on my couch: It's my favorite evening throw in the winter because it is as thick as fur and the hair is waterproof. An assortment of keys my mother left behind in my house became my jewelry.

Have you ever wished you could trade in your life of glamorous eccentricity for one of dreary conformity?
I strongly believe my eccentricity was spawned by my ability to the make use of whatever things were at hand at the time. I love to make do. Making do makes a great do. I once wore my hair—it's down to my waist—as a top belted into pinstripe pants.

When does eccentric glamour become idiocy?
When it is being noticed. Oh, dear!

Who is your inspirational icon of glamorous eccentricity?
I have two: Joey Arias and Diana Vreeland.

Do men think you are hot?
Ruben does, and that is good enough for me! Regarding men: When I first understood the psychology of clothes, I started to dress to keep the "wrong" type of guys away. But the simpler I dress, the more I get approached. I once wore a pair of jeans and sneakers on the subway and never did that again because of how approachable and vulnerable that suddenly made me. A bit of eccentric glamour keeps the wrong kind of men away.

What is the thing that most offends your glamorously eccentric sensibilities?
The whole concept of "being cool."

Where do you wish to be buried, and in what?
I will levitate into nonexistence—wearing the feeling of AIR!

CHAPTER 5

Call Ghost Bustiers

Exorcising your vintage clothing

In the delirious quest to live a life of eccentric glamour, the Gypsies and Existentialists among you will undoubtedly find yourselves donning dead people's clothing. I'm talking about secondhand garments. Vintage.

While the typical Socialite is much too neat and prissy to buy clothes at flea markets—she comes out in a rash just thinking about it—you Existentialists and Gypsies do not really have a choice. Your whole point of view is contingent upon augmenting your wardrobe with the kind of unique and eccentric pieces that can be found only at vintage emporiums.

Though I am a huge proponent of the creative recycling inherent in vintage shopping, I would like to offer a word of caution. No, I'm not talking about fleas or horrid aromas. And I'm not about to rail on for pages about the fact that much of what is labeled "vintage" is merely out-of-date schlock that is barely five years old. These issues, though burning, lack the urgency and gravitas of the one I am about to address.

I am talking about stuff of a more supernatural nature.

I'm talking about ghosts.

Think about it. How can you be so sure, when you purchase that taffeta mambo dress, that it is free of the energy and spirit of the former owner? How can you be sure that you are not buying a ghostly Gucci or a haunted Halston?

The answer is, you cannot.

It happens innocently enough: You snag yourself a little vintage Valentino—Julia Roberts picked up her Oscar in an old Val and didn't look half bad—for the upcoming office party. You are pleased as punch. You know you will be the only gal in the room thus attired. In your smug self-satisfaction you have overlooked an important fact: The frock is completely impregnated with the spirit of the previous owner. It's veritably dripping with ectoplasm.

Though agnostic/atheistic in many regards, I have a healthy respect for ghosts. Always have.

When I was twelve years old, a lady in our neighborhood kicked the bucket. She wasn't actually much of a "lady," but the word "lady" was randomly applied to adult females back then.

The next day, the local housewives descended on her bungalow, grabbing booty left and right, each claiming that various of the deceased's personal effects had been promised to her. One particularly assiduous scavenger who, for the sake of anonymity, I shall refer to as Blanche, managed to nab a nice set of teacups and an attractive floral sundress.

Blanche was shorter than the deceased. No matter; Blanche was an expert seamstress. So before you could say "bust dart," she had donned her wrist pincushion and, with the frock dangling on a hanger in her living room doorway, embarked on a hasty alteration.

She had nearly finished pinking a full four inches off the hem (she intended to make it into what used to be called a self-belt, i.e., a belt made of the same fabric) when the garment started to twitch violently on the hanger. Within seconds, a powerful poltergeist turned that tubby little frock into a demonic funnel of whirling fabric.

Blanche screamed blue murder and ran out into the street. It took hours of soothing persiflage to persuade her to reenter her house. Two hours later, accompanied by a caring friend, she crept back inside.

"There are no spirits lurking in that frock. It was just a draft. You'll be fine after a nice cup of tea," said the unsuspecting pal.

Inside the house, everything was still. By the time the kettle had boiled, a tentative normalcy had been restored. A nice cup of hot, sweet tea! This miracle beverage had always seen the Brits through the best and worst of times. This occasion was no exception. Or was it?

Blanche raised the lid of the teapot. The brew was well steeped and ready to be drunk. With her hand still shaking slightly, Blanche did the honors.

"Sugar?"

"Ta, luv. I'll help meself."

The two ladies cringed slightly and smiled apologetically to the heavens as they realized, simultaneously, that they were about to drink out of the dead lady's teacups. After exchanging philosophical glances, they raised the cups to their lips. This action was closely followed by a stereo scream as both ladies realized that the freshly brewed tea had *turned ice cold . . . in the dead lady's cups!*

Needless to say, Blanche dropped off her booty at the Salvation Army thrift shop the next day. The story became an urban legend in my gritty little hometown. When last heard of, Blanche had gone a bit strange and moved to an undisclosed location.

Why am I telling you this story?

For the last decade, I have watched couture-crazed fashionistas gobbling up vintage clothing with a cavalier and naïve disregard for the paranormal potential lurking in those Puccis and Fioruccis.

The truth of the matter is that spirits and ghosts of all varieties love a nice bit of *schmatte* as much as you or I. Garments are wondrous relics that have lingering spiritual and metaphysical ties to their original owners. Dubious? Do the words "Shroud of Turin" mean anything to you?

For those of you who think I may have lost my mind, let me reassure you that my observations are based on in-depth, rigorous scientific research. These lengthy experiments were conducted with the aid of a professional medium named Joe Trolly. A former missionary, philosophy professor, and professional roller-skating puppeteer, Mr. Trolly provides spiritual advice and cosmic connection to a broad range of New Yorkers.

Our forays into the paranormal not only confirmed my darkest suspicions, they gave me lots of great tips on how to buy vintage without incurring the wrath of any wraiths. Mr. Trolly, a conservatively dressed, white-haired, avuncular Wizard of Oz–like bloke with a quietly flamboyant and ironic personality, conducted our first experiments at a Greenwich Village vintage store named, appropriately enough, Resurrection, and located on the site of a former funeral parlor.

This store had some choice items of clothing with formerly famous owners. To Mr. Trolly I offered, for his cosmic delectation, a jacket that had been owned by Jimi Hendrix. Without hesitation he declared this jacket to be "clean."

Closing his eyes and breathing deeply, he elaborated, "It doesn't need an exorcism. The spirit has departed without any problems. Jimi knew how to travel in the cosmic sense." How true!

Our second experiment involved a rack of early Ossie Clark dresses. I wasn't surprised when my medium started picking up some histrionic vibes. Ossie, the designer for the jeunesse dorée circa 1970, was knifed to death in a Joe Orton–style boyfriend murder in 1996.

Mr. Tolly attempted to calm Ossie's agitated spirit.

"Eeeuuoooweesh! This spirit is very angry—but not about the murder. He's angry at the lack of talent in the fashion world today, and he is frantically channeling his creativity through today's designers—filling the *horrible void*—from the other side." This shockingly accurate observation (at the time of this exorcism, vintage Ossie Clark designs were the biggest single influence on the pastiche-filled fashion landscape of the early twenty-first century) neutralized any doubts I may have had about my theory.

Mr. Trolly moved quickly to an A-line velour printed Pucci skirt. At first, I thought he was wincing at the $850 price tag. I was just about to tell him that this was actually a very good price for vintage Pucci when he started communicating with "the other side." "Very negative energy," he declared, holding the garment at arm's length, "Anyone who buys this skirt should be warned. She will need to perform some kind of ritual, even if it's hanging the skirt out to air on a washing line. If a negative person buys this skirt, it could intensify her negativity."

Mr. Trolly, who looked as if he was about to start projectile vomiting key lime pie, dumped the treacherous skirt on the counter and ran to the other end of the store, where he impulsively grabbed another garment.

"This person was interfered with at a young age," he said, protectively cradling a navy blue men's velvet jacket. He continued, "Not sexually. His development was arrested—it happened to Prince William, too—by getting too much attention. It can stunt your spiritual growth. Wait! This person is not dead . . . and . . . I think I can help him!"

I looked inside the jacket and saw an Yves Saint Laurent (gasp!) label. Mr. Trolly was talking about Yves *lui-même*, the genius who hurtled into the spotlight at the tender age of nineteen and paid a heavy psychic price. For the second time, Mr. Trolly had sidestepped the mundane former wearer and gone right to the glamorous designer. He clutched the jacket and began sending some fabulous, fuzzy energy to Yves.*

The exorcisms and channeling continued.

Our tireless research bore fruit. The conclusions can be summarized as follows:

(a) Do-it-yourself: When faced with the need to exorcise, you do not need the services of a professional medium. The most mundane solutions are the most effective: Dry cleaning, according to Mr. Trolly, gets rid of bad spirits.

(b) On an obvious note, buying more recent vintage—'80s or '90s—can reduce the likelihood of a vicious haunting, because the original owner is probably still alive.

---

* Since the Trolly exorcism, Monsieur Saint Laurent would appear to have attained a place of greater personal contentment. Coincidence? I don't think so.

(c) Good spirits inhabit clothing just as often as nasty ones. If you bought some of Julia Child's old pantsuits, you would be bound to pick up some of her optimistic bonhomie. Maybe your cooking would improve.

(d) Sharing and caring: When a good spirit manifests itself in that Dior cocktail dress, don't rush it to the Martinizing center. Even if the frock in question has a whiff of stale fragrance or vintage BO, you must allow the spirit to linger. You must share the frock with that friendly spirit.

(e) Be a vulture: If you hear that a famous fashion plate is about to pop her Blahniks, you would be well advised to start circling and keep a close eye on the obituaries. When a well-dressed lady goes to the big sample sale in the sky, there is invariably a feeding frenzy. You want to make sure you get dibs. That said, pulling up in front of the house with a rolling rack in tow before the body is cold is bad taste and will annoy the dead spirit. You don't want to end up like Blanche, do you?

*"Every eccentric is used to whispers,
finger pointing and giggles.
It comes with the territory."*

MR. MICKEY BOARDMAN

Deputy editorial director of Paper *magazine,*
wearer of twinkle-knit sweater sets, and one of New
York's best-loved fashion eccentrics responds to the
Eccentric Glamour questionnaire.

What are you wearing?
Dries van Noten leopard-print track jacket over a hot pink ladies' sparkle top from eBay. Chocolate brown Marni trousers,
Missoni socks, and sparkle flats from Forever 21, which were a
gift from a friend.

**When did you first realize that you might in fact be a
glamorous eccentric?**
When I was about four years old I was obsessed with my mother's favorite look: a wide-leg pant and matching floor length
vest worn over a bishop-sleeved blouse, often with some kind
of secretary tie at the neck. She loved to wear them with very
high cork or wood platforms.

In terms of my own look, moving to New York in the late

'80s was critical. I discovered thrift stores and flea markets and even found clothes on the street. Although I was very fashion forward in high school—wearing ladies' designer jeans long before Karl Lagerfeld—I was certainly not applauded for my style. In New York, people went crazy for my looks, which encouraged me to reach new heights, or depths, depending on your perspective.

Were your parents horrified?
My mother hates two things more than anything. One: when I wear vintage clothes. She says, "Do you want people to think we're poor?" Two: When I wear ladies' clothes.

My parents were always very concerned that I might be gay and they were horrified when I wore eye shadow at nine years old. But it *never* would have occurred to me to carry a ladies' handbag or wear a ladies' top in those days. Even now I don't do it as a drag or gender thing. I just think the ladies' tops are cuter, and I like a form-fitting look, not a baggy man look.

Are you prone to mood swings?
I'm mostly manic, but I can have depressive moments. But I usually snap out of it pretty quickly.

Have you ever been mocked for any of your glamorous eccentricities?
Absolutely. For years I never rode the subway in New York when I was running around in crazy looks because although the looks created a sensation in the clubs or at Fashion Week or with fun people, the average fool on the street could be very confused or hostile. Once when I was wearing a Lilly Pulitzer pant and coordinated Lurex top and sparkle vest ac-

cessorized with a straw bag from the Bahamas and straw flip-flops from Pearl River, a construction worker accosted me and said, "You're dressed fuckin' funny," and not funny ha-ha like he liked it. I said, "I have a mirror at home. I know how I'm dressed."

Of course, every eccentric is used to whispers, finger pointing, and giggles. It comes with the territory.

What is the most eccentrically glam thing in your closet?
I have a full-length black and silver . . . I don't know what to call it . . . maybe a dressing gown or hostess coat. It's soooo glamorous!

Have you ever wished you could trade in your life of glamorous eccentricity for one of dreary conformity?
Never. In days gone by when I'd be harassed or mocked, I'd feel very self-conscious and wonder if it was worth it. I'd also cross the street if I saw a bunch of straight boys coming, but in the end I love the attention even if it's bad. And at this point in my life and career I've gotten so much positive recognition for my taste that anyone could laugh in my face and I'd still feel immensely secure in my fashion choices.

When does eccentric glamour become idiocy?
It's such a thin line. In the old days I would be walking to work and literally my look would fall apart on the street. Everything was held together with a safety pin or the seams would be busting and just unable to hold my big man frame in their little lady garments. I'd get to work and not have pants on.

I also find that idiocy creeps in when you don't have time to really get things together and you go with something that is untested. That's why it's best to stick with your signature looks for the important things, I think. Still, I cherish moments of fashion idiocy and think you sometimes have to risk looking like a fool to really make the magic happen.

Who is your inspirational icon of glamorous eccentricity?
Lynn Yaeger [fashion writer for the *Village Voice*] is pretty much the poster girl for glamorous eccentricity. Her look has *nothing* to do with trends or wanting to get laid, the two things that I think most sabotage great fashion.

The same goes for Isabella Blow, although I think she really wanted to get laid, which was kind of problematic considering how she dressed. It takes a special kind of man to want to stick it in the girl in the Philip Treacy lobster hat.

Anna Piaggi [legendary Italian fashion editor] is also a maverick. Some of the things she does are so experimental that I honestly don't understand them, and I feel like I'm pretty advanced, so I cannot begin to imagine what the man on the street must think.

Do men think you are hot?
I feel like my fashion choices ruin any chance of being seen as sexy. So many of my friends have outfits they wear for festive occasions and then outfits they wear to get laid in, and I just don't delineate that way. It was very complicated in the old days when I'd meet guys on phone sex lines and then show up at their house in a ladies' bodysuit under polyester pants and plastic rain boots. Not very sexy, I'm afraid. But at the same time, maybe someone did think I was sexy. Maybe I did not believe it myself. I probably either scared suitors away or didn't notice their interest.

What is the thing that most offends your glamorously eccentric sensibilities?
Laziness when it comes to fashion, and I'm guilty of it myself. I think everyone should always go overboard with their looks and everyone should only wear things they think are fabulous. I can't believe that all the people who dress exactly like the people around them think that their clothes are fabulous. For me sequins make every day a red-carpet event. I think people should wear gowns every day, or hot pants in the winter, or Kabuki makeup to the supermarket. I so worship and respect anyone who really puts in that effort to always have a look together. Even if it's a dirty, East Village junkie look. I just applaud the commitment and when I make the effort I feel sooo rewarded in many different ways.

Where do you wish to be buried, and in what?
I want to be cremated, but I'd like to have the chicest memorial service in history. I don't own anything black (except the silver and black sequined hostess coat I mentioned earlier and some black A.P.C. pants I got at a sample sale), but I *adore* couture funeral looks. Nothing is more chic than a royal funeral with queens and princesses all in veils and widows' caps. I'd also like it to be black tie so there would be tons of jewels involved. I want tiaras over the veils, full orders, ribbons, evening gowns, etc.

I want to be laid out in an open casket wearing a custom-made sparkle ensemble. Maybe a tuxedo that's embroidered with sparkles. Maybe Louis Vuitton or Chanel couture for men. Something sick and wrong.

I'd want to have very subtle false eyelashes and a schmear of lip gloss. I'd want everyone weeping hysterically and hurling themselves on the casket.

Then I'd be cremated and scattered in the creek at Val-Kill, Eleanor Roosevelt's home where she ran amok with her lesbian sidekicks. I wouldn't want the bejeweled mourners to know I'd be scattered there. I'd want them to think I was scattered on the Dalmatian coast or at Baltic alongside Queen Marie of Romania's palace on the Black Sea.

CHAPTER 6

Aunt Sylvia's Fanny Pack

A career à la mode

As you set about the task of crafting an individual look and expressing yourself through the garments that you throw on your back, you may find yourself getting irritated. You may find that the quest for an eccentrically glamorous wardrobe, the adorning of your body with intriguing raiment, leaves you cold. You may find that you have about as much interest in fashion as your fanny-pack-wearing lesbian aunt Sylvia. No problem.

This is perfectly fine with me.

Your style indifference does, however, make you less of a glamorous eccentric and more of a plain old eccentric. Think of it this way: Marlene Dietrich was a glamorous eccentric, but Eleanor Roosevelt, Janet Reno, and Big Edie Bouvier were just plain old eccentrics, i.e., norm-breaking gals who were disinclined to creative personal adornment.

Please note: Being an unglamorous schlumpy eccentric is infinitely preferable to being an unglamorous noneccentric, or even a glamorous noneccentric. (Think of those gussied-up trophy wives whose idea of sizzling conversation is to say things like, "You simply cannot get a bad meal in Itlay.") The eccentric part is the real deal breaker. Eccentricity, that vigorous aversion to preconceived ideas and bourgeois notions, is the oxygen that invigorates a happy and creative life.

Which brings us back to your lesbian aunt Sylvia. She is a primo example of a nonglamorous eccentric. Though she has, in all other aspects of her existence, always been a wacky chick, she has never felt the inclination to express her eccentricities via her appearance. Sylvia knows her limitations: She knows that she is physically incapable of walking in rhinestone-encrusted Louboutin burlesque pumps, and that if she wore them on her Vermont bird-watching trips they would sink into the mud.

I have no desire to foster burdensome and inauthentic Louboutin addictions in those whose interests lie elsewhere, and whose door keys, wallets, cell phones, and tampons are happily stuffed into fanny packs. If you and your aunt Sylvia can find contentment only when you have all your possessions bulging at your abdomen, then far be it from me to divest you of your favorite accessory.

On the other hand . . .

You may find the absolute opposite. You may find that the quest for eccentric glamour impels you to unclick that fanny pack forever, catapulting you into a genuine love affair with fashion.

You may find yourself becoming instantly completely and utterly fashion-crack-addicted.

You may take to it like a transvestite to marabou.

You may go way beyond merely adopting a more glamorously eccentric personal style and become hopelessly infatuated with the world of fashion.

You may you find that, after dabbling your tootsies in the waters of la mode, you are so enamored that you elect to change the course of your life. Suddenly you are looking for a career in the rag trade.

Having been partially responsible for instigating this life change, it seems only fitting that I provide you with some tips on navigating the pitfalls and idiocies of this magical but sometimes depressing world. Yes, I said depressing.

This is going to sound insane, but the biggest mood swings I have ever had in my entire life occur during New York Fashion Week. And they are getting worse. As with every passing season the hype and the hoopla get bigger and the number of shows increases, my mood swings are becoming more and more pronounced.

"Oh," I hear you saying, "you are just a blasé old burnout who has habituated to the fabulousness of it all and should probably hang up your Blahniks and buy yourself a fanny pack." Not true! My fashion enthusiasms are, even after thirty-five years in the business, as fevered as ever. Nothing—I repeat, nothing—gets me more excited than the sight of a hip chick or bloke strutting about in an innovative, well-designed, alluring ensemble. Every season, twitching with optimism, I charge off to Bryant Park in the hope of seeing such things. And then the mood swings start.

Here's the problem: As I enter the tents I am set upon by hordes of fashion groupies and hangers-on, all braying at me about their soon-to-be-launched clothing lines or online newsletters and/or shoving their self-congratulatory résumés into my available orifices. This is surely the same genre of lottery mentality loony who swarmed at the gates of old Hollywood studios in search of unspecified satisfactions.

The following tips are designed to prevent you from becoming one of the above-described demonic Eve Harringtons.

Your First Runway Show

Attending a fashion show for the first time can be a bewildering experience. Though your lesbian aunt Sylvia may be a dab hand at unblocking her compost toilet or changing the tire on her pickup truck, she will have no useful advice on how to conduct yourself in this particular situation. But I do. Here are some pointers to ensure that you maximize the moment.

Snacks Growling stomachs. I hear them all the time during the course of New York Fashion Week, where the schedule leaves little time for eating, and the sole purpose of the ear-splitting music is to mask the sound of the aforementioned growling. Bringing sugary doughnuts, smelly hot dogs, and oversized pretzels to fashion shows is, therefore, an excellent idea. I endorse it. I support it. I applaud it. People eat at baseball games. Why not serve food before every fashion show, à la sports stadium?

Maybe the reason that fashion people are all a bunch of food-disordered freaks, and that people like Aunt Sylvia have a more laissez-faire attitude toward food, is that Aunt Sylvia, working as she does as the manager of a health food restaurant, is simply around food more often.

Increasing the ubiquity of food in the fashion milieu might significantly help to combat the deranged superskinny trend that is currently wreaking havoc on the bodies of so many models and actresses. If the Council of Fashion Designers of America wants fashion folk to develop positive eating habits—or any eating habits at all—it needs to integrate food onto the runways. There is absolutely no reason why Diane von Furstenberg herself—the CFDA president—could not push a big stinky hot dog cart down the catwalk while we wait for her show to begin. ("More relish, Anna dahlink?") Instead of perfume in those goody bags, why not a piping hot chipotle burrito?

Adulation Always go backstage! From Marc Jacobs to Oscar de la Renta, every designer's worst nightmare is *not* being mobbed after his or her show. Nobody is too low down on the totem pole to participate in the après-show air-kissing festival. Not even Aunt Sylvia! (She can always gain entry by claiming to be a security guard.)

Fake adulation Love a particular designer but hate the clothes in his or her show? Should you be brutally honest, or should you perjure yourself? Here is my solution: When it comes time to gush with the backstage compliments, I simply shriek, "You've done it again!" at the top of my lungs and keep walking.

Pushy galore Though it is absolutely not okay to rush up to people like Donna Karan and Karl Lagerfeld and start hounding them for employment—you demonic Eve Harrington, you!—it is perfectly appropriate to discreetly shove a copy of your résumé into their purses when they are not looking.

Charity Giving your fashion show ticket to a homeless person living in Bryant Park is civic-minded and otherwise highly commendable. Don't forget to give the chosen vagrant your name, and remind him or her to take full advantage of the freebie cologne in the gift bag. Who doesn't love a fragrant vagrant?

Becoming a Fashion Critic

As you enter and leave a fashion show, random representatives of the media will assail you for your opinion on the collection. Chances are that you, with your total lack of experience, will have no idea how to rate what you saw.

If you want to know whether or not a collection sucks, you have to look for subtle clues:

Postmodern bunk Read the press release before the show. If the designer in question is touting postmodern themes, e.g., Barbie goes to Chechnya or Cyberslut meets Imelda Marcos on acid, this is a sure sign that all might not be well in the atelier. This kind of mumbo-jumbo is a clear indication that a designer may be overly focused on wacky, hype-generating concepts. Earth to designers: Women cannot wear abstract concepts; they can only wear clothes.

Colonial chic If the collection in front of you reminds you of those mind-numbing historical tableaux you yawned through during a childhood trip to Colonial Williamsburg, there could be a problem.

Kitchen witch chic If, when the models begin to walk the runway, they remind you of an inanimate household object, such as oven mitts, trash bags, or kitchen witches, this is a clear indication that something is wrong.

Danglers In the old days, a dangling hem or a fraying seam was a sure sign of failure. This is no longer the case. Deconstruction—raw seams and sawed-off sleeves—is ubiquitous. Now the situation is reversed: If a designer's collection has perfect top-stitching and immaculate seams, the collection is probably a dud.

Hootie blows If you are enjoying the sound track more than the clothes on the runway and the sound track is Hootie and the Blowfish, alarm bells should sound.

License to kill If the designer in question has reached the point where he has licensed or sold his name to a big corporation, then keep your eyes on the guys in gray suits in the front row. If any of these gentlemen is openly weeping or gulping down cyanide capsules, this indicates that the collection might be less than fabulous.

Stampede Keep an eye on how fast Petra and Natasha are walking. If the models break into a cavalry charge—those thoughtful hussies are trying to spare you the pain of actually seeing what they are wearing—you can assume the worst.

Fire sale If the designer comes out to take the curtain call and starts handing you flyers for an impromptu backstage sample sale—starting immediately—this is a sure sign that the garments are barking.

The ultimate litmus test?

Take every single outfit on the runway and imagine your aunt Sylvia wearing it with her fanny pack. If she looks amazing in even one outfit, then you know that you are mistaken and that the designer in question is, in fact, a total genius.

Starting Your Own Company

It may turn out that you have real megatalent. If people are constantly stopping you on the street and asking, "Where can I buy a raffia cocoon coat like that? Does it come in magenta?" or "Who designed your Zouave pantaloons? They're so great," you just might have what it takes to head up your own company. You may be one of those rule-breaking glamorous eccentrics—Madeleine Vionnet, Coco Chanel, Vivienne Westwood, et al.—who, in the search for self-knowledge and creative fulfillment, have changed the course of fashion and make stupendous amounts of cash in the process. Cross your fingers and adhere to the following dos and don'ts.

Crystal balls Do not, whatever you do, gouge money from your parents' 401K to pay for your first runway show. It is extremely hard to succeed in the world of fashion. You may never make enough money to pay back the ma and pa, or you may lose your mind and become a crystal meth addict, and then what? When you have emptied their bank account, and they are old and toothless and living in a homeless shelter, you will feel really, really guilty.

Parasite Don't let the fact that you cannot afford to have your own fashion show get in your way: Why not promote your own collection by staging guerrilla shows on the sidewalk outside other people's shows? All the press and glitterati will have a chance to view your creations and you, the parasite, will save a fortune on show production costs. Be prepared for a certain amount of hostility from the "host" designer.

Freebies are verboten Do not give away your frocks to overpaid movie actors who can easily afford to buy them and will appreciate you and your designs far more if you actually force them to open their huge bulging purses and pay for them. No graft!

A chair is still a chair . . . Always play Burt Bacharach while you are working on your collections. Burt's menthol-cool musical stylings will soothe your shredded nerves and promote creativity.

Create! Be original! Knocking off crap from the thrift shops is very last century, dahling!

Mass with class Don't be an elitist! Working at Kmart can be just as fabulous as working at Maison Lanvin. It requires more creativity to make middlebrow, Middle America look glamorously eccentric.

Don't play God Never try to be good at everything. You are not omnipotent. You're not J-Lo. Instead of trying to become the next Giorgio Armani, carve out a niche for yourself. Pick a neglected area and reinvent it: Sweaters, brassieres, evening wear, men's tailoring, foundation garments, jockstraps, brunch wear—pick a category and stick to it!

Thin and thinner Never hang out with fashion models. You will just become dumber and dumber. Most people are really boring when they are in their late teens. Models are no exception. Conversational topics among these lovelies range from broken fingernails to alarm clocks that didn't go off, causing flights to be missed.

Seek out the company of hideous wrinkled old sages, former demimondes, fiery pedants, and brilliant intellectuals. These are the people who have the ability and the backstory to expand your frame of reference.

Give Aunt Sylvia a job Last but not least, do *not* employ other glamorous eccentrics. If you are lucky enough to get to the point where you have burgeoning business and you need help, then you must employ only very serious, boring, hard-working, earnest people. No Eve Harringtons! *You* are the star!

And if you need a fit model? There's much to be said for pinning everything on fanny-pack-wearing Aunt Sylvia. If your designs fit her eccentric body, they will fit anybody.

"My mother was appalled. She threw me
in the back of a cab, hoping nobody would
recognize us. But I didn't care because I was
having my first love affair with style."

PROFILE

IRIS APFEL

Part Queen Theodora of Byzantium, part Nancy Cunard,
a major textile designer and expert whose style is so unique
it has been immortalized in a massively influential exhibit
at the Metropolitan Museum of Art in New York responds
to the Eccentric Glamour questionnaire.

What are you wearing?
A hip-length, boxy, A-line jacket by Geoffrey Beene, double-face and reversible in gray and a fabulous blue—almost a cornflower blue. Chrome yellow, very narrow suede trousers. Pucci print boots, above the ankle, with a black patent cuff and heel, anchoring my huge black glasses.

Round my neck I'm wearing a whole mess of huge beads, Baltic and African amber with some Bakelite mixed in and some blue-gray feathers I found in Venezuela. Bracelets? Tons and tons and tons. On both arms.

When did you first realize that you might in fact be a glamorous eccentric?
When I was eight years old I was taken to get a photo portrait

done. I decided to pose as a dancer and swathed myself in diaphanous draperies à la Isadora Duncan. Not such a great look on a chubby gal.

Were your parents horrified?
My mother was appalled. She threw me in the back of a cab, hoping nobody would recognize us. But I didn't care because I was having my first love affair with style.

Are you prone to mood swings?
I'm pretty even. But I have them once in a while. It's part of my entitlement package.

Have you ever been mocked for any of your glamorous eccentricities?
I once got hate mail from some jerk in Miami about my glasses. He even put his address. But most people like my look.

What is the most eccentrically glam thing in your closet?
Me. It's not that my clothes are so eccentric. It's the way I put them together.

Have you ever wished you could trade in your life of glamorous eccentricity for one of dreary conformity?
That would be a big fat no-no!

When does eccentric glamour become idiocy?
All too often. As Harold Koda [head of the Met's Costume Institute] always says, "It looks easy but please don't try this at home." If people have no sense of who they are, experimentation can be a disaster.

Who is your inspirational icon of glamorous eccentricity?
I never really had one. I wish I did; it would have made my life easier. But that's why I did it all myself.

When I was a kid, I loved Rosalind Russell. I remember some movie where she charges into her office—smothered in silver fox "flings" with heads—and she runs to her desk and starts answering three phones at once. Fabulous! And Pauline de Rothschild. Years ago I saw a spread on her called "Life in a Draughty Chateau." There she was head to foot in YSL. And she always had such great boyfriends—John Huston, Edward Murrow. And I admired Millicent Rogers. She wore Mainbocher and Balenciaga with jewelry bought from Indian chiefs— huge chunks of turquoise.

Do men think you are hot?
At eighty-five I'm lukewarm. When I was younger I always had lots of offbeat gentlemen callers. The good ones were not turned off by my look. And now I have Carl. Fifty-nine years together. He's cute and cuddly and he cooks Chinese. What more could a girl want? And he's a gentleman. He wouldn't take anyone's eyeballs out for a buck. And we laugh. You might as well be dead if you cannot have fun.

What is the thing that most offends your glamorously eccentric sensibilities?
People not being themselves and trying too hard—an old bag shouldn't wear a miniskirt. There are other ways to have youthful esprit.

Where do you wish to be buried, and in what?
I would rather stick around.

CHAPTER 7

Looking Cher

Tempus fugit, so get used to it

"If you can convince yourself that you look fabulous,
you can save yourself the trouble of primping."
—*Andy Warhol*

A skin-care saleslady at an unnamed department store is trying to sell face cream to passers-by. Nothing unusual or
pernicious about that, you might say. But when nobody pays
any attention to her spiel, she ups the ante. A hidden camera
catches her telling potential buyers that the jar she is holding
"has just won a Nobel Prize."

A few blocks away a New Age beauty company breaks new
ground in the already excessively gimmicky world of cosmetics promotion by offering "long-distance Reiki treatments" to
clients and press.

Downtown, a beauty company announces the launch of a
new skin cream with a historical spin. According to the press

release, the recipe comes from Roman times and replicates that of "the world's first skin cream."

Across the continent in LA, celebrities are slathering their faces with a brand new unguent containing human skin cells cloned from babies' foreskins. "Increased elasticity," so say aficionados, is the desired outcome.

In Malibu, a movie star gets wind of the fact that certain Sunset strippers and pole-dancers are now bleaching a certain orifice. She follows suit.

What's my point?

Oh, nothing much, really. Just that the entire world—the beauty industry in particular—has gone *stark-raving mad*!

As a card-carrying glamorous eccentric, you are obliged to swim through this incomprehensible sea of sticky lotions and notions espoused by prophetlike beauticians. You must acquaint yourself with the current scene. In doing so you will see things—as per the Charlene song—that "a woman ought not to see." You will come face-to-face with this sick world of bleached sphincters and babies' foreskins.

Don't shy away. In order to navigate this madness you must understand the various trends that are currently driving the beauty and skin-care industry.

Let's break it down:

First, there's the let's-make-it-seem-like-teams-of-scientists-created-this-cream trend.

The overarching aesthetic of this movement is very Dr. Strangelove/Dr. No: Sinister salespeople in crisp lab coats man these particular cosmetic counters and try to get your business by hurling scientific jargon at you about antioxidants and alpha-hydroxificationism. A cursory glance into their eyes will reveal that they have no idea what they are talking about. Like the crews on porn films, these folk have long since habituated to the content of their jobs and are thinking about their lunch.

Next trend.

With a *ching* of finger cymbals and an "om" or two, we move on to the mystical trend.

This trend is *huge*! I have yet to meet someone in the beauty industry who is not capable of introducing the word "spirituality" into a conversation about mascara. With its endless talk of auras and energy cleansing, this is definitely the most entertaining trend.

When they are not casting runes, New Age beauty practitioners are balancing their chakras. In this wacky woo-woo crunchy world, even lip gloss and eye cream are imbued with cosmic meaning. This has led me to posit the theory that the superficiality of one's job is directly proportional to one's "spirituality." Think about it: You never hear of a construction worker or trauma surgeon insisting on "sage-ing" his work environment before getting down to business. The bottom line? The more you surround yourself with face creams, the more likely you are to become a shaman of some description.

Ching! Next.

At the opposite end of the spectrum from the mystical trend we have the flagrantly unspiritual if-porno-stars-are-doing-it-then-so-can-I trend.

Yes, this is where the Evas of the world—the pillow-lipped Carmen Electra wannabes referred to in Chapter 1—find the materials to craft their look. This trend involves lots of spray tan, Botox, superdrippy lip gloss, hair removal, and moderate amounts of pain. Aficionados are the world's chief consumers of lip liner.

This trend is closely affiliated to the most popular beauty trend of all: if-movie-stars-are-doing-it-then-so-can-I trend.

This trend involves the most pain, cost, and inconvenience and is therefore the most incomprehensible.

A movie star has a totally legitimate reason for freezing every nerve in her face, sucking every fat cell from her body, slicing and dicing her face and irrigating her colon until it sparkles.

If she doesn't, she will get fired.

If she "lets herself go"—who among us has not secretly harbored the desire to kick off those mules, grab the gin bottle, and let ourself go?—the phone will stop ringing and she will end up flat broke. Left with little or no alternative, the celeb chick tortures herself with horrid injections and nasty procedures.

The delusional identification with movie actors has caused many people to subject themselves to those same tortuous Hollywood beauty treatments: "If Reese Witherspoon is getting a skin peel with lighter fluid, then so am I," is the thinking.

Overlooked is the fact that if Halle or Renée does not stay young looking and fabulous, she will lose her entire income source. You will not. You can work at your office job until your boobs and jowls hit your computer keyboard and nobody will ever fire you. You have a million reasons to increase the eccentric glamour of your appearance but none to flagellate yourself like an A-list celeb with needles and colonics and fat injections.

So why do the ordinary women in the street subject themselves to these kinds of self-punitive, costly, time-consuming procedures? Can it be explained by that all-powerful overidentification with red-carpet celebs?

The answer is simple and rather obvious: These women, like the followers of all of the above-listed masochistic trends, are terrified of getting old.

Growing Old Ungraciously

I'm a gynocrat. I wish that women ruled the world. I view women as superior to men. They are funnier and more intuitive. They can cook. They have a high pain threshold. They rarely start wars. They blow disposable income in places that have consistently provided me with a steady income for my entire adult life. Yes, there's much to be said for the female of the species.

With regard to their attitude to aging, they are, however, in dire need of a little male perspective.

While you ladies are overly focused on antiaging regimens, we men are more laissez-faire. While there are some idiot fellows who are subjecting themselves to Botox and calf implants, the majority of men accept the inevitability of decay without putting up too much of a fight.

This is a healthy thing.

We humans are all doomed to wrinkle, wither, and die. When we are young we have tight pretty skin. When we are old we get wrinkly. *C'est la vie!*

Accepting the inevitability of your physical decay—or, at the very least, cultivating a masculine indifference to it—will allow you to enjoy life and to revel in the eccentric glamour of every waking moment. If you can reconcile yourself to the fact that you will, eventually and inevitably, morph into a hideous old crone, you will enjoy your pretty years much more.

I once heard Olivia Newton-John—one of Australia's leading thinkers—tell a reporter that her biggest regret in life was fretting about how she looked when she was young. "I was so gorgeous, but I was too busy looking for signs of aging to enjoy it," was the gist of her spiel. She wasted time and tainted her gilded youth by obsessing about wrinkles.

The ladies who are attempting to hold back the sands of

time with Botox injections, lipo, boob-lifts, and babies' foreskins are not just wasting time and money. They are deluding themselves.

In their deranged minds they think that all those expensive procedures and products are turning back the clock. They aren't. They cannot. Nobody gets to go to the prom twice. The sweet bird of youth is not a round-trip shuttle.

The horrible truth of the matter is that these cosmetic addicts, despite their best efforts, do not look youthful. They look taut and frozen. At worst they look Jocelyn Wildenstein. At best they look Cher.

Looking Cher is a new phenomenon. Neither young nor old, happy not sad, the Chers of the world have invented a new and, dare I say it, plastic way to look.

(Dear Cher, This chapter is not a diss. You are a major glamorous eccentric, a role model of self-empowerment and general kookiness. And *looking Cher* is very different from *being Cher*. Your particular cosmetic odyssey, though excessive for a nonceleb, is entirely understandable. You are a performer—an Oscar winner, no less!—who did whatever it took to survive for decades in the looks-ist culture of Hollywood. Long live Cher!)

Looking Cher is enigmatic. It's hard to describe. It's void of emotion. The only thing you can definitively say about the women who look Cher is that they do not look like they would if they had not had all that stuff done.

Looking Cher, though it makes perfect sense for an entertainment celeb living in a youthcentric culture, has two principal drawbacks.

(1) If people don't know or cannot tell your age, they will have no choice other than to ask: "Hey, Mavis! How old are you?"

If, on the other hand, your life is written across your face à la Golda Meir—see how far back I have to rummage in order to get a good example of an uncut iconic face!—people will not need to ask your age or bamboozle you into revealing it by hurling trick questions about the Great Depression, the Dust Bowl, the French Revolution, or the Mayflower.

(2) When people aren't sure of your age, they will add rather than subtract. Permit me to explain using Cher as an example: The "dark lady" has been looking eerily youthful for so long that everyone has lost track of her age. This, unfortunately, does not work in Cher's favor: Cher, and those of her ilk, have been hoist by their own petards. Why? Because when ordinary folk cannot figure out how old you are, their tendency, when speculating, is always to err on the ungenerous side. That's just how we humans are. When Cher turned sixty, everybody said, "My God! I know she looks about twelve years old, but she has been looking youngish for so long, I had completely lost track of her age. I assumed by this time that she was about ninety-five."

Madonna, same thing. Madge throws herself around like a sixteen-year-old. Ten years later she does another tour and hurls herself across the stage again, with, other than the occasional knee brace, no discernible sign of aging. Her fans shriek, "Wow! She's still at it at sixty-five." Meanwhile Madge has not hit fifty yet.

It's a biblical thing: If you succeed in making yourself look much younger than you are, people will stare at you with open mouths as if you have just come back from the dead. Lazarus, *bonjour!*

If you continue, over a decade or two or three, to look age nonspecific, people will eventually start to think you are phenomenally old. *Bonsoir*, Methuselah!

Reducing the Appearance of the Appearance of the Appearance of the Appearance of Fine Lines and Wrinkles . . .

What happened to the days when a smidgen of lipstick and a dab of Arpège were all you needed to feel like a movie star? For some reason the emphasis of the beauty industry has shifted to increasingly complex skin care/skin torture and away from the simplicity of those good old-fashioned maquillage basics.

It's time to shift it back.

Here's why: First, skin care, with all its pseudoscientific babble, is boring! It is utterly yawn making to read the endless labels and try to figure out what a particular product is supposed to do to your skin. Applying them is even more boring. Rubbing creams under your eyes in order to "reduce the appearance of fine lines and wrinkles" is neither rewarding, amusing, nor aesthetically exciting. You would have much more fun and get much more immediate results learning how to glue on showgirl lashes or apply a beauty mark.

Second, skin care is a bunch of lies. Give any doctor or dermatologist a couple of martinis and he or she will admit that topically applied unguents are useless. The whole nature of the epidermis is that it is impregnable. You might be able to "reduce the appearance of fine lines and wrinkles," but you will still have those "fine lines and wrinkles." You will merely have "reduced" their "appearance," whatever the hell that means.

Bottom line: A cheap drugstore moisturizer is all you need.

(If you have a thing about petrochemical products, then try olive oil!)

Third, skin care doesn't really work. I have friends who go to the top facialists in the world and the "appearance" of their "fine lines and wrinkles" is exactly the same as "the appearance of the fine lines and wrinkles" on the toothless lady who lives in a box on my block in Manhattan.

There is only one reason for slathering on eye creams and blowing your cash on neck and facial unguents: because you enjoy it and it *feels good*, especially when you do it in bed. As Andy Warhol said, "Everything is more glamorous when you do it in bed, even peeling potatoes."

The moral of the story: Ease up on the skin care and spend more time slapping on lipstick, foundation, eye shadow, and mascara.

Makeup Is Good For You

A friend of mine—an ex–ballet dancer named Imogen—never left the house without full makeup. With her huge belashed eyes, prominent cheekbones, and pale face, Imogen was the perfect Existentialist. Her dramatically maquillaged face was in a perpetual state of *Swan Lake* readiness. Pancake and lashes and the whole bit. After years of slapping on foundation and powder, you would expect her skin to be a mass of clogged pores. It wasn't. It was downright flawless: decades of "slap"* had protected her skin from pollution, London fog, and her endless fag smoking.

---

* Slap: English vernacular for makeup.

Shake Up Your Makeup

If you are still dithering about whether you are a Gypsy, an Existentialist, or a Socialite, the smartest thing to do is to let your God-given features guide you. Don't fight your shortcomings. Let them be your signposts. Examples:

- Plump redheads make great Gypsies and lousy Socialites.

- Skinny, pale, haughty-looking chinless gals make great Socialites, passable Existentialists, and lousy Gypsies.

- If you have dark circles under your eyes, it's probably genetic. Embrace it and incorporate it into an Existential German Expressionist look. Think Liza Minnelli in *Cabaret*. Think Otto Dix!

As with your fashion, it is important that your maquillage be a form of personal expression that gives you creative satisfaction. There are, however, some basic dos and don'ts that apply to each type.

Beauty and the Gypsy

Do concentrate on your eyes. Daub your lids with Renaissance colors: maroon, burnt orange, olive green. A little metallic, a little shimmer? Why not?

I strongly advise Gypsies to stay away from liquid eyeliner: Though kohl is traditionally a very Gypsy-ish thing, I find that you Gypsies lack the concentration to apply it in liquid form. I recommend that you leave it to the Existentialists, who are more anal-retentive and have better hand-eye coordination. Don't forget to block: Since you Gypsies spend a lot of time skipping around alfresco in an artsy kind of way, always make sure you have gallons of SPF in your carpetbag.

Beauty and the Socialite

You are polished, you are glamorous and, unlike the Gypsy, you are a gal whose look is most reliant on a well-tutored hand. You, more than any other gal, are in dire need of a trained homosexual to apply your makeup. If you do not have the wherewithal to hire one, simply endear yourself to one of the nice fellows who flits around the MAC or Vincent Longo counter at your local department store.

Beauty and the Existentialist

Rouge your ears, just like Diana Vreeland!
Do think Kabuki. *Do* think graphically, as in black, red, and white. *Do* learn how to glue on fake lashes. *Don't* buy loads of crap: Find a good mascara and a pale foundation, and stick to it. Black Existentialists should take their cue from Grace Jones: Apply blue or metallic highlights to your cheeks and dye the inside of your mouth red with a drop or two of red food coloring.

'Til Death You and Your Lipstick Doth Part

Let's end with a universal tip for Existentialists, Socialites, Gypsies, and all combinations thereof:

Your thirtieth birthday is an important landmark. You are now ready, after ten years of dicking around with your personal style, to select a signature lipstick. This is the lip color that will be with you through thick and thin.

When you are screaming for mercy during childbirth, this is the lipstick that will be smeared across your face.

When you kiss the corpses of your dead parents, this is the lipstick that will stain their cheeks.

If, God forbid, you ever get arrested for drunk driving, this is the pigment that will leave a pretty residue on the Breathalyzer nozzle.

This is the lipstick that will flow into *the fine lines and wrinkles* around your mouth as the death rattle grips your throat.

Choosing this lipstick is therefore a momentous task.

In order to complete it, you need to be slightly drunk.

After a Cosmo or two, head to your local beauty counter and start trying out the lipsticks on your hand. Just for kicks, why not ask if any of the lipsticks has won a Nobel Prize? Don't expect to have some kind of epiphany when you find "the right one." Your selection should be, within reason, fairly arbitrary. If it has a great name—Catfight (Nars), Sashimi Mimi (MAC), or Pink Ballerina (Chanel)—and doesn't make you look too hideous, then that's probably good enough. It's just important that you pick one and stick with it.

When you have made your choice, buy a total of three hundred and sixty lipsticks. (The alcohol helps numb the pain of having to cough up all that dough.) This stash will last you the next sixty years. Yes, Einstein, that's six per year.

That crate of lipsticks, lurking in your closet, will never let you forget that the clock is ticking and that life is for living. Every time you extract a new one and propel it toward your naturally aging mouth, you will think of the pointlessness of trying to hold back the sands of time. That diminishing lipstick stash will be a constant and salutary reminder not to waste time dating crappy men, watching lousy television, working dreary jobs, or worrying about the appearance of your fine lines and wrinkles.

Have a nice life!

"*A bitchy, undermining, and blond eighth-grade 'friend' told me that I was 'no Christie Brinkley' but was 'sort of . . . exotic.'*"

ALEXANDRA JACOBS

*Writer, New York Observer editor, book critic, wife
of comedy writer Jon Bines, and mother of emerging
glamorous eccentric Josephine Bines responds to the
Eccentric Glamour questionnaire.*

What are you wearing?
An unintentional pastiche of post–World War II optimistic sportswear: navy cashmere 1950s cardigan with a Saks Fifth Avenue label; blue-and-white-striped 1960s narrow-cut knit T-shirt made by a surely long-defunct West German company; brown 1970s Levi's Sta-Prest pants (I have a weakness for English language–mangling brand names); a 1940s sterling-silver charm bracelet with, among other items, a miniature toy soldier, telescope, cocktail shaker, torpedo and—somewhat incongruously—a thimble. The shoes and underpinnings are from the twenty-first century.

When did you first realize that you might in fact be a glamorous eccentric?
When a bitchy, undermining, and blond eighth-grade "friend" told me that I was "no Christie Brinkley" but was "sort of . . . exotic." (N.B. This was Manhattan, not Peoria.)

Were your parents horrified?
More like oblivious.

Are you prone to mood swings?
I'm prone right now, having one.

Have you ever been mocked for any of your glamorous eccentricities?
Yes, by *you*, Simon. Remember the turquoise and cream crocheted stole I wore to Bottino during my all-too-brief "pom-pom phase"?

What is the most eccentrically glam thing in your closet?
My 1950s leopard-print coat from enokiworld.com—everyone has a version of that now, but not with a label inside reading Sidney Blumenthal, like the former *New Republic* journalist and adviser to Bill Clinton. I like to whip it open and impress political types.

Have you ever wished you could trade in your life of glamorous eccentricity for one of dreary conformity?
This must be why I still shop at the *Gap*.

When does eccentric glamour become idiocy?
When someone goes into debt for it.

Who is your inspirational icon of glamorous eccentricity?
Diana Vreeland, even though she wore basically the same thing every day (right?).

Do men think you are hot?
Ask my husband.

What is the thing that most offends your glamorously eccentric sensibilities?
Punk rock.

Where do you wish to be buried, and in what?
I want to be cremated, then stored in aforementioned husband's favorite piece of architectural pottery or scattered in Central Park.

CHAPTER 8

Who Killed
Joie de Vivre?

Squeeze a lemon on the cat and shout, "Sourpuss!"

You wake up in a foul mood. You had that nasty dream again, the one where you are squatting in the corner of an empty white room eating your own hair.

To cheer yourself up, you squeeze your legs into a pair of black-and-white striped opaque tights. (Stylewise, you are definitely an Existentialist. You love graphic hose and avant-garde fashion by obscure Belgian designers. You even have a collection of bizarre prewar foundation garments.)

The striped leggings do not improve your mood. You feel like a clown/idiot/mime from the moment you leave the house.

At lunchtime you run out—in a blur of striped leggings—to get a manicure. At your request, a Korean lass, whose name is Misty, paints your nails a dark gloss forest green. You feel better. Something about the green nails makes the leggings more successful. On your way back to work, an old homeless person who looks a bit like God yells something unrepeatable at you. You have another mood swing.

Now the day is over. You're waiting for the bus in the rain. Your hose are splashed and soggy, and so is your psyche. Another day of seemingly pointless toil is over.

What you need is a quiet evening of self-love and pampering to restore your faith in humanity. You order take-out dumplings from your favorite restaurant and then—now comes the most important bit—you stop at the newsstand to pick up a pile of this month's fashion magazines.

There's nothing quite like flicking through a pile of glossies while stuffing your face to restore a girl's joie de vivre.

Or is there?

You lock yourself in your room. You munch. You peruse. You munch. You flick. There's Gisele Bündchen lying sprawled on her back in a double-page spread clutching a designer handbag. She seems like a nice girl, but she looks a trifle pissed off in this picture.

Here's a group of models lolling in a hayloft looking totally drained after doing God knows what. Flick the page.

The advertising and the editorials are chock-full of impossibly beautiful lads and chicks striking languid attitudes in zillion-dollar outfits and sucking in their cheeks.

What do they all have in common?

They all look acutely *unhappy.* Sullen. Miserable. Annoyed, even.

This seems so illogical: After all, isn't fashion supposed to be upbeat and groovy, a dash of *Abfab* and a dollop of Holly Golightly? Isn't fashion supposed to be *fun?* Yet the pampered lovelies in your glossies do not appear even remotely amused. Far from it. They all look as if they just got their test results back from the doctor. The diagnosis is not good. Now they are preparing to die a lingering but gorgeous death.

Munching frantically, you search for more uplifting images. Flick! Flick! Something. Anything! Flick!

More ridiculously skinny people looking down their noses . . . at you! Flick! Why did you fork out your hard-earned money to be condescended to by a bloody magazine? Flick! More articles about pompous, haughty people living fabulous existences in palatial houses to which you know you and your leggings will never be invited. Flick! Sheesh! There are more smiling faces in the average medical catalog than in these fashion periodicals. By the time you get to your horoscope, your mood is darkening again: You seriously contemplate hanging yourself with your own carnival hose.

Tossing the mags aside, you grab your mouse. How about a bit of online shopping? Maybe that will cheer you up.

The landing pages of the luxury fashion websites are filled with the same joyless images. www.morose.com. Every model looks as if she wants to bitch-slap somebody or slit her own throat or both. She may be festooned with sparkling jewels or swathed in a brightly colored designer frock, but her mood is black. She might just as well be wearing a burlap sack for all the fun and joy she is extracting from all that pricey raiment.

But why?

Why is it that luxury + fashion = misery? Why do so many fashion magazines make you feel like poop? Why can't these periodicals be warm and communicative—and human!—instead of exclusionary, cold, and elitist?

Why are being happy and being cool deemed to be mutually exclusive concepts?

While we try to figure this out, let's take a trip to a fashion show. Surely there will be some joie de vivre here.

Backstage at Bryant Park is a sea of laughter, excitement, and glamour. This is more like it! That playful creativity and collaboration that makes fashion such a fun career is raging full throttle. Frantic last-minute fittings, hairdos, and maquillage create an atmosphere of modish, madcap Mardi Gras. Here are all those po-faced models from your magazine pages, but they are barely recognizable.

Why?

Because they are actually enjoying themselves.

And, guess what? They look ten years younger for it. Giggling and goosing each other and quaffing champagne, they laugh and gossip in various Eastern European languages, the very essence of jeunesse dorée.

Then the show starts and the laughter stops.

Once these Chechen chippies get out on the runway, it's a whole other story. The models, now looking much older, give the impression that they are walking, albeit defiantly, to the guillotine.

Why do they look so morose? They have no cause to be miserable. They are young and gorgeous and lissome, and even a second-string gal gets paid infinitely more than she would toiling in the copper mines back in Estonia.

So why aren't they skipping? Why aren't they shrieking with laughter at their good fortune?

The lack of jollity and the relentless stomping—where did that ridiculous walk come from?—makes for an unrelentingly grim spectator experience.

Why do those in charge assume that because something is expensive it has to be presented in such an angry, humorless way?

Why is *fun* so anathema to the world of high fashion?

What would happen if Karl Lagerfeld started dating Phyllis Diller?

Here's my theory:

At some point in our recent history—maybe it was during the Kurt Cobain-smelly-Nirvana-unwashed-sock period of the early '90s—jollity went out of style. The Isaac Mizrahis, Jean Paul Gaultiers, and Todd Oldhams of the world—all brilliant combiners of fashion and humor—moved to the back burner of fashion.

The emaciated waif supplanted the sensuous, smiling glamazon. Almost overnight, fun went out of style. It became hip to be glum.

Seasons passed. Kurt shot himself. The angst-ridden '90s progressed, and a dour minimalism became the norm. Fashion became "intellectual." The notion that only stupid, dorky people have fun became woven into the fabric of every Helmut Lang blouse and Martin Margiela trouser.

Despite the fact that it has long since lost its original frisson, this exuberance-free vision of la mode continues unabated to this day. The few remaining fashion designers—Betsey Johnson or Heatherette—who relentlessly inject overt humor into their presentations have a hard time being taken seriously.

Let's take back the frivolity!

I refuse to accept the idea that *style* and *humor* are two mutually exclusive concepts. As a result, I have embarked on a mission to make fun cool again, and vice versa.

My waking hours are now dedicated to injecting a bit of humor into the world of fashion. At Barneys, where I have worked for more than twenty years, our marketing mantra speaks for itself: TASTE LUXURY HUMOR. As much as I love a novel frock or an innovative blouse, my absolute favorite thing on earth is to watch people—thin, fat, fashionable, unfashionable, homeless—chuckling at a Barneys window or giggling over the copy lines in a Barneys ad.

As you set about the process of creating a more eccentrically glamorous you, you are bound to increase your exposure to the montage of potentially souring cooler-than-thou fashion imagery described above. You will need to have your wits about you in order to navigate this world of tight-sphinctered pretentiousness. Please, I beg of you, let no day pass without reminding yourself that the glumming down of fashion is both illogical and counterintuitive.

Oh! The utter pointlessness of a life without fun!

Only an idiot would accept the mandate to feel grim and dour after forking out hard-earned cash for trendy clothes or glossy mags. And you are not an idiot. You are a courageous rule breaker who is on a transformational quest. You are in the process of rejiggering your image, and there is no point in attaining your goal unless you are having fun.

How to Have More Fun

Ditch the Politesse

"I like to be the right thing in the wrong place
and the wrong thing in the right place . . . Being
the right thing in the wrong place and the wrong
thing in the right place is worth it because something funny always happens."

—*Andy Warhol*

An exaggerated sense of occasion, or any sense of occasion, for that matter, will automatically impede your ability to have fun. Conversely, a well-cultivated obliviousness to the conventions of any occasion is guaranteed to up the fun quotient.

When people ask me, "What are you wearing to [such and such event]? I'm not sure what to wear . . . ," I experience a strong desire to kill them. These whiny people, with their obsolete sense of appropriateness, are the Antichrist.

Because of their irrational and fun-destroying fear of being either overdressed or underdressed, they are attempting to create a world where, on any given occasion, all participants are uniformly attired.

I deplore this idea. The impulse to surround yourself with like-minded folk in like-minded frocks signifies the end of civilization. I want every social event to be like the happening in the movie *Midnight Cowboy*, or better yet, the party scene from *Beyond the Valley of the Dolls*. Rampant individuality are my buzzwords. If every social event were to showcase a fabulous smorgasbord of humanity—duchesses and drug addicts, artists and bankers—the world would be a more entertaining and therefore happier place.

And to the conformity freaks who are trying not to offend the great unseen fashion god in the sky, let me reassure you on this issue: Your concerns about dressing "appropriately" are totally misplaced. Nobody in his or her right mind really cares enough about what you are wearing to censure you. If there is such a person on the planet, then he or she—this self-appointed arbiter of "appropriateness"—deserves to be confronted with as many "inappropriate" transgressions as possible.

And what, while we're on the subject, could possibly be more fun than encountering someone who is "inappropriately" dressed? A pink satin frock at a funeral, a tiara for a Monday morning meeting—these are a few of my favorite things.

Back in the 1980s there was a senior buyer at Barneys who had a reckless disregard for convention. She was an Existentialist of the first order. Every day I anticipated her arrival at work with jittering eagerness. One never knew what she was going to wear: a severe antique Chanel suit with a massive nineteenth-century bow on her head, a silk faille cocoon coat in slate gray with matching beaded ballet slippers. Hers was a delicious form of style schizophrenia. She would think nothing of wearing a floor-length ball gown to a nine a.m. store managers' meeting.

She enjoyed dressing up, and everyone looked forward to seeing what her next outfit would be. It was *fun*. The idea of "work wear" or "career clothing" was repulsive to her, as it is to me.

(At this juncture, the pedants among you will be flicking back to the first chapter where I declared that professional women—MDs and lawyers in particular—must never wear wacky clothes, and accusing me of inconsistency. To you nit-pickers, I say: (1) The young lady in question was not a gastroenterologist, she was a fashion buyer, and (2) Stop being so pedantic.)

Retire Your Work Attire

London, 1978.

There I was, standing in the gloom of the sordid hovel I happily shared with a cross-dressing cabaret entertainer named Biddie. We were living *la vie bohème*.

I was panting.

In the middle of the floor was a Matterhorn of rumpled garments. They were my clothes. All of them.

Having accepted a window-dressing job in the United States, I was now attempting to pack before heading west in search of a better life. It was all very *Grapes of Wrath*, the new-wave version.

Having tried repeatedly and unsuccessfully—hence the pant-ing—to jam that Matterhorn of garments into two ratty suitcases, I was going nowhere fast. Clearly, some editing was in order. I glanced across the room at my roommate's closet. What a hideously disorganized transgender hellhole it was! Men's and women's clothing battling it out for space on a single rolling rack. And yet, upon further inspection, I saw that there was indeed some method to the madness. It was, albeit roughly, bi-sected by gender. The chiffon dresses were up one end and the tweed suits were up the other.

This gave me an idea.

I began by dividing my clothes into two groups. I dubbed one pile WORK and the other FABULOUS.

The work group comprised dull basic items: jeans, sweaters, dungarees, flannel shirts, and T-shirts. These were my schlep-ping clothes, garments that, if spattered with paint or ripped by nails, would not be lamented.

The fabulous group comprised my party clothes. These garments—punk couture, sharkskin suits, fluorescent shirts, brothel-creeper shoes, and new-wave neckties—were the clothes I wore when I was shrieking and boozing and going to Bowie concerts and to the *Blitz* to watch my roommate perform with his singing partner, whose name was Eve Ferret. These were the clothes I wore when I was having *fun*.

Looking at the two piles, one so associated with grinding toil and the other with euphoric reward, I began to ques-tion the validity of this self-imposed system. I suddenly saw it for what it was: the fashion equivalent of having a "special" room—the nicest one in your house—that contains plastic-covered couches and is used only on "special" occasions and, as a result, hardly gets used at all.

There was something sad about the fabulous pile: It contained many rarely worn garments that I had been overly concerned to preserve: That blue and white satin jockey jacket—it sounds hideous but it was madly au courant during the glam-rock era—was now embarrassingly out of date. I had worn it twice. What a waste!

Before you could say "gold lamé toreador slacks," a solution presented itself.

Stock shot of plane leaving Heathrow.

Stock shot of plane arriving at LAX.

Stock shot of people arriving at customs. One person appears to be having much more fun than the others. *C'est moi!*

I had left all the work clothes behind and packed only the fabulous clothes.

The moral of the story: Every day is a special day. A tear in your chiffon? So what! A food stain on that satin ruffle? Big deal! A little paint spatter on that velvet blazer merely adds to your overall patina.

When women ask me for fashion advice, I always say the same thing: "Go home and throw out all your 'work' clothes!"

If you always dress as if you are going to a party or a Bowie concert—or a Black Eyed Peas concert—you will always have more fun.

The Blue Death

Among the discards on that floor, back in old Blighty, were several pairs of jeans. I was glad to see the back of them. There was nothing special about them. Jeans were what people wore on the occasions when people did not care what they wore.

Back then in the late 1970s, who could have predicted that a mere thirty years later, the world would be in the grip of a veritable denim plague?

I call it the blue death.

The denim trend, which swung into action in the late '90s with the boot-cut, butt-crack craze, has gone on too long. Far too long.

In the counterculture 1960s, denim jeans were associated with pleasure and leisure: Woodstock, *Easy Rider*, etc., etc. How paradoxical that these once-transgressive garments are now, half a century later, sucking the inventiveness and fun out of dressing up.

Denim has become a disempowering standby.

The result: A horrible conformity is raging whereby the entire earth's female population—not just the Evas derided in Chapter 1—is squeezing its collective ass into denim jeans of one brand or another and teaming them with a floozy tank top or halter. This phoned-in, homogenizing look is a corner-cutting device, a shortcut to cool, which reeks of faux bohemia and will jeopardize your ability to attain any acceptable level of glamorous eccentricity.

Don't be lazy.

If you put all your jeans in a bag and drop them off at Goodwill, you will force yourself to seek out alternatives. You will automatically gain in individuality. You will find yourself wearing a sequined Mexican dirndl (Gypsy) or black gabardine gauchos (Existentialist), and you will automatically have more fun. I'm talking good clean wholesome fun sans stimulants. Which brings us conveniently to . . .

My Gray Teeth

I have a drug/booze theory—not a popular one, I will admit— that people who are incapable of having fun without getting smashed or high do not really understand fun. They have

SIMON DOONAN

bought into a contemporary Hollywood/Lindsay Lohan/Paris Hilton version of fun. The cocktails and coke-snorting night-life. If I sound like a Jehovah's Witness, well, I am, sort of.

For years I never dined, discoed, mingled, or frolicked without getting thoroughly smashed. I was lubricated. Well-oiled. One night in the early '80s, I rolled home from either the Palladium, Area Club, the Pyramid, Danceteria, or possibly all four and began babbling incoherently at Robert, a nontransvestite roommate, about what a simply faboo time I had had and how simply beeeeeyond Iman looked and Dianne Brill this and Andy Warhol that and blah blah blah. I suspect I might have been eating a bowl of cereal at the time.

Robert, I should explain, hails from Carlisle in the north of England, where people have a wonderful tradition called plain speaking, also known as Northern plain speaking. It's the English working-class equivalent of "telling it like it is."

After listening to my repetitive drunken braying for about five minutes, and watching cereal and names drop from my lips, my pal, a reformed abuser of long-standing, let me have it.

"You're slurring like a drunken old fishwife. You smell like a barmaid's apron, and your teeth are a heinous gray color from drinking red wine," he hectored, adding, somewhat unnecessarily, "and you're a mess!"

Something about this caring intervention touched a nerve.

I felt as if a gauntlet had been thrown down: "You are incapable of having a good time without getting snot-slinging drunk," his challenge seemed to say.

I ceased boozing on the spot and have not touched a drop since.

For more than twenty years I have navigated the social whirl of New York while stone-cold sober. This has been, and continues to be, a very amusing experience. As much fun as life was when I was guzzling booze, it is fifty times more hilariously surreal without the anesthetizing benefits of alcohol. It was only after giving up booze that I came to understand the true nature of fun: Fun is infantile.

Fun is about playing Twister or Ping-Pong.

Fun is about being unsophisticated.

Fun is about embracing embarrassment and owning it.

Fun is about dorky things like Renaissance fairs where you can wear your striped leggings without fear of being mocked.

Fun is running up to the Russian embassy, knocking on the door, and shouting, "Hello! Is Len in?"

Fun is bringing a tambourine to work.

Fun is learning to play the theremin and then giving concerts to the funsters at the neighborhood old folks' home.

Fun is about squeezing a lemon on the cat and shouting, "Sourpuss!"

Fun is about enjoying fashion and not venerating it.

Fun is doodling mustaches on those dour fashion magazines with a big fat Sharpie.

"I am, in point of fact, a dork."

MALCOLM GLADWELL

*Bestselling author, he of the exuberant Afro and
Thom Browne suits, responds to the Eccentric Glamour
questionnaire. (Like all male heterosexual glamorous
eccentrics, he is in deep denial.)*

What are you wearing?
Levi's. Some kind of striped shirt and a gray jacket I bought on
Greenwich Street.

**When did you first realize that you might in fact be a
glamorous eccentric?**
I hate to break it to you, but I don't consider myself either eccentric or glamorous. I am, in point of fact, a dork—something my
friends have realized (and mercifully kept to themselves) for years.

Were your parents horrified?
My parents actually do find me glamorous. But that's because
they live in a very small town in rural southern Ontario. They
would find me glamorous if I lived in Rochester.

Are you prone to mood swings?
Almost never. In fact, almost nothing—even recreational drugs—can shake me out of my normal placidity.

Have you ever been mocked for any of your glamorous eccentricities?
Quite the opposite! I suspect that my friends snicker about my boringness behind my back. I remember when I first met my friend DeeDee Gordon, who really is a glamorous eccentric, and she looked at what I was wearing (as I recall, an ill-fitting black jacket) and actually rolled her eyes. That was my first encounter with DeeDee: an eye roll. It's been downhill from there.

What is the most eccentrically glam thing in your closet?
I have a velvet jacket that I bought, in a moment of insanity, in SoHo. I wore it once and felt so excruciatingly self-conscious that I've never worn it again. I'm about to give it to the Salvation Army.

Have you ever wished you could trade in your life of glamorous eccentricity for one of dreary conformity?
You mean—be even *more* boring? Not likely!

When does eccentric glamour become idiocy?
Really tough for me to say. I regard all those who are higher up the fashion food chain than me with undisguised awe. There is no idiocy in my book. Only greater and greater degrees of daring and panache.

Who is your inspirational icon of glamorous eccentricity?
No contest. Brian Eno. I met him once and was speechless the

entire evening. All I remember is that he spoke in perfectly formed paragraphs. You could have transcribed his dinner table conversation and published it verbatim. Now there's a true glamorous eccentric! He gave me his email address afterward and told me to contact him, but I was too chicken. Oh well.

Do women think you are hot?
I have no idea. I hope so.

What is the thing that most offends your glamorously eccentric sensibilities?
Again answering hypothetically, white sneakers? The nonathletic wearing of track pants? Any sort of T-shirt or sweatshirt with an Ivy League college on it?

Where do you wish to be buried, and in what?
Believe it or not, I love Bobst Library at NYU more than just about anywhere. I'd like to be buried in the current periodicals room, maybe next to the unbound volumes of the *Journal of Personality and Social Psychology* (my favorite journal). Ideally, people would have to step over my grave to read the latest issue. What would I be wearing? God knows. Maybe a Toronto Maple Leafs hockey jersey. That's my hometown. Go, Canada!

CHAPTER 9

Frenchwomen
Don't Know Diddly

Vive la vulgarité!

Frenchwomen are so fabulous that they can smoke loads of Gitanes without getting bad breath or brown teeth.

Frenchwomen can eat croissants without getting crumbs on their cashmere cardigans or worrying about cholesterol or becoming hideously obese.

Frenchwomen always take off one accessory before leaving the house.

Frenchwomen understand how to keep their men happy in special secret Frenchy ways, which sometimes involve black lingerie.

Frenchwomen can tie an Hermés scarf on their heads and not end up looking Kurdish, not that there's anything wrong with looking Kurdish.

Frenchwomen put lavender in their panty drawers.

Frenchwomen are so bloody perfect and superior it's annoying.

Frenchwomen are full of chic!

I'm driving through Miami Beach and I'm feeling ridiculously chirpy. Who doesn't love Florida? Florida is happy and gaudy. Florida is cheery and garish and unpretentious and American. Florida is proof that a dollop of vulgarity is as uplifting and life-affirming as a dose of Zoloft.

I switch the radio dial to NPR.

"If I 'ave a little dessert at dinner, maybe I say *non* to ze croissant ze next morning."

It's that spokeslady for all things French, Madame Mireille Guiliano, and she's is being interviewed about her wildly successful book *French Women Don't Get Fat.* Her lightly accented voice is quietly confident, imperious, some might say.

"If I eat ze croissant or brioche in ze morning, zen no dessert."

There is something peculiarly French about the calm superiority with which Madame Guiliano offers up her pearls of wisdom to the American public. The subtext of her message is clear: Permit me, *s'il vous plaît*, to prevent you vulgar Americans from turning into a nation of total *cochons.*

As I engage more with the content of Mireille's interview, I realize that it is, especially in the context of NPR, profoundly mundane. Despite the gravitas of her delivery, all she is really doing is advising us to refrain from stuffing our gobs with excessive amounts of food. The content of her message seems a trifle obvious. How is she getting away with it? Who decided that this fancy broad had the requisite gravitas for a lengthy spot on the *Diane Rheims Show*? It's hard to escape the feeling that La Guiliano got booked for the show simply because she is French. If she were American, nobody would care what she ate or when.

As I listen to her pronouncements, I try to imagine the chorus of bewildered yawns that would greet a midwestern housewife if she went on National Public Radio and doled out similar tips.

Mrs. Average: "If I overdo the ambrosia salad at night, then I always hold back on the Entenmann's the next morning."

But Mireille is not from the Midwest. Mireille is French. So she has *la carte blanche* to blather on about all kinds of boring Frenchy things.

I'm sure she is not deliberately trying to bore us. Her agenda, and that of so many French know-it-alls before her, is more subtle and complex. It is as follows: I, Mireille Guiliano, am asserting my cultural preeminence by comparing you gargantuan, undisciplined junk-food-eating Yanks to me and my fellow Frogettes. We have finesse and restraint. You do not. Drawing attention to this fact gives me great pleasure. It is my favorite pastime.

Mireille's NPR talk got me thinking about Frenchwomen and their role as style yardsticks in the lives of we ordinary non-Frenchies.

Why, oh why, are we so enamored of *les Françaises*?

They have tyrannized us for centuries with the dreaded notion of the faux pas, which, by the way, is the lethal archenemy of eccentric glamour. A faux pas is to a glamorous eccentric what a peanut butter sandwich is to somebody with a raging first-degree nuclear peanut allergy. Not good. The whole intent of the faux pas is to inhibit any glimmerings of the rule-breaking impulse that is the basis of eccentric glamour.

So why do we hang idiotically on their every word, as if

they know so much more about style and general fabulousness than we do? How did all these fag-smoking madames and mademoiselles manage to coax us all into this state of pathetic, incontinent, jibbering, masochistic insecurity?

In the interests of fairness, let's look at a couple of the positive things the French have given the world.

First and foremost—a personal favorite of mine—we have the obscure concept of *chien*. The nuanced use of the word *chien*, though it has been around for decades in Paree, has never crossed the Atlantic. This could also have something to do with the fact that every time a French bloke vocally admires the *chien* of an American visitor, he gets his face slapped.

What the hell is *chien*? The literal translation is "dog.*"*

My translation? Chien = eccentric glamour!

When the Frogs say a woman has *du chien*, they do not mean to imply that she is a dog. *Au contraire!* They mean that she has something very special that sets her apart from the crowd. Impertinent, irreverent, slightly bitchy, a tad mysterious, nonbourgeois, charming, self-invented, good at applying eyeliner, amused, and above all nonconformist, the mademoiselle with *chien* is a fabulous confection of style, self-empowerment, and black patent sling-backs.

If you want to get a real eyeful of *chien*, take at look at some of the groovy French movie stars of the last century: Brigitte Bardot, Fanny Ardant, Isabelles Adjani and Huppert, Jeanne Moreau, Jane Birkin, Zizi Jeanmaire, Simone Signoret, Juliette Gréco, Françoise Hardy. *Bonjour!* The list is a long one. Even the more homely broads like Claude Pompidou and Edith Piaf had an idiosyncratic style. But all these illustrious ladies are all *d'un certain age* or pushing up the daisies. Where are their equals today? They would appear to have no contemporary equivalents. Open a French magazine *d'aujourd'hui* and all you will see are pictures of American tabloid queens.

So why, given that the Deneuves and Moreaus would appear to have no successors, do the French still have our marrons glacés in such a viselike grip?

I can't help thinking that Coco Chanel has something to do with it. Somehow, even thirty-five years after her death, the haughty, highly quotable ghost of Coco Chanel has the ability to reach down (or up) and create waves of self-loathing in non-Frogs. Her voice lives on in her famous aphorisms.

"Elegance is refusal" is surely one of Chanel's best-known and, truth be told, strangest sayings.

Petite problème: What the hell does it mean?

Nobody knows and nobody seems willing to ask. When we ordinary folk encounter this bewildering statement, all we can do is wince and retreat to the shameful inelegance of our non-French, unrefused lives. Nobody dares to ask the obvious question: Refusal to do what, exactly, Madame Coco?

Refusal to take out the garbage?

Refusal to wear a rainbow Afro wig?

Refusal to be less horribly French?

Refusal to eat a tuna melt?

Refusal to say what exactly one is refusing to refuse?

Nobody seems to have any idea.

This, by the way, is classic French tactic: By being oblique and incomprehensible, the French keep us all in a jittery state of oppression.

Much as I would love to blame Madame Chanel for our pathological reverence for all things French, I think there might be another woman—an American!—who is even more culpable. I refer to Judith Krantz.

In her worldwide blockbuster *Scruples*—over six million

147

copies sold—La Krantz vaunts the mystical superiority of the French.

Here's the story: The heroine, one Honey Winthrop, is "a good child with a kind heart, though not much of a heartbreaker." She is ripe for a duck/swan transformation. This, according to La Krantz's plotline, cannot possibly happen as long as she stays Stateside. Honey's metamorphosis begins only after she alights on French soil and waddles into the clutches of the mysterious Comtesse Lilianne de Vertdulac.

La Comtesse is a shabby-chic aristo who, having fallen on hard times, takes in genteel paying foreigners from good families, teaches them to speak French and oh so much, much more. Krantz describes La Comtesse as follows: "Her style was a mixture of innate taste stripped down to its simplest expression and a personal evasiveness, a quality of holding herself back, eluding intimacy, which gave her that fascination which forthcoming people never inspire."

So here it is in a nutshell: When people are jolly and open and friendly (i.e., American) they lose out. Who ends up in the driver's seat? Who gets to pull the strings? The dour and unforthcoming people of the world! The French!

Needless to say, La Comtesse, with her watery soups and impeccably cut suits, successfully transforms Honey from "a baby hippopotamus" into an unimpeachably chic replica of herself. Our heroine returns to America where, armed with her flawless sense of (French) style, she snags a rich husband and becomes a retailing legend. The implication to the zillions of Krantz readers is clear: Get your ass over to Paris and start soaking up the ambience or resign yourself to a tawdry life of trailer parks and Dairy Queens. *Quelle horreur!*

While conceding that France has produced a breathtaking torrent of culture and fashion, I must confess that I have always found French people slightly off-putting, sinister even. We are, after all, talking about the people who invented not only the guillotine but also "the French wash" (trans: sloshing cologne on your body in lieu of a more complete ablution).

In the meantime, what's to be done? How do we stop them?

Why are they—the very same race that invented the concept of *chien*—trying to impede the development of our eccentric glamour and make us all feel that the worlds of style and taste were peppered with land mines, the location of which was unknown to everyone except French chicks? How do we get the French down off their high horses and into the gutter along with the rest of us? How do we divest ourselves of this need to feel inferior to them in matters of style and fashion? How do we instigate a characterological change in the French?

Here's a possible solution: According to Madame Mireille Guiliano, the average French woman is so fabulously disciplined that, shockingly, she does not eat between meals. *Rien!* Nothing!

No beef jerky. No Cheetos! No Fritos! No midmorning snacks for her!

Though this restraint is obviously a huge factor in the maintenance of those youthful French figures, I think there is more to the story: Might not this overly anal-retentive attitude to cuisine and diet be the reason why Françoise and Brigitte and Solange are always so bad-tempered and disdainful? Are they not merely grumpy because they are hungry?

There's no question that small portions—combined, of course, with a serious commitment to Gauloises—can keep obesity at bay, but I suspect that such a lifestyle might have serious emotional side effects. We're talking major mood swings. Think about it! It makes perfect sense. Hungry + thin = svelte + grumpy.

No wonder they are always vaguely annoyed. Put yourself in their position: Wouldn't you be a tad irate if everyone around you was chomping on Cracker Jack and Pirate's Booty and you couldn't have any because you were French?

It is my firm belief that, by introducing the Frogs to American snack foods—Nutbutters, Pringles, Lorna Doones, and the like—we may be able to take the edge off those brittle Gallic personalities and create some common ground. Simply put: The French could benefit enormously from a dollop of our fast-food vulgarity.

Vulgarity is the key!

Mireille has got it all wrong.

We do not need their help. They need our help and our Cheetos and our vulgarity.

Vive la vulgarité!

When Coco Chanel, who was probably lighting up her hundredth fag of the day at the time, said, "Luxury is the absence of vulgarity," she was attempting something very wicked. She was trying to give vulgarity a bad name. I cannot help feeling she was also simultaneously attempting to option the rites to the idea of *good taste* on behalf of French women for all eternity!

Naughty Coco! Bad!

She should not be allowed to get away with it. Let's storm the Bastille and take back *la nuit* and turn the tables on the Frogs and show them that we, the great people of America, can be luxurious and vulgar all at the same time, all while eating a massive bucket of KFC.

Liberté! Fraternité! Vulgarité!

Hit the streets! Spread the word! If you meet any resistance, subdue your opponent with a quote from the very American Diana Vreeland: "Vulgarity is a very important ingredient in life. A little bad taste is like a nice splash of paprika. We all need a splash of bad taste—it's hearty, it's healthy, it's physical. No taste is what I'm against."

Put that in your bong and smoke it, Madame Coco!

"Open-toe sandals with too long nails and a French pedicure with rhinestones. Eeeuw!"

KELLY WEARSTLER

Star of Top Design, *the chicest and most eccentrically glamorous interior designer since Elsie de Wolfe responds to the Eccentric Glamour questionnaire.*

What are you wearing?
A Doo-ri top, Hysteric Glamour jeans, Lanvin flats, and a Solange Azagury-Partridge ring. It's Sunday, so I'm in my flea-market-scouring outfit.

When did you first realize that you might in fact be a glamorous eccentric?
When I began dressing my teddy bear Frank in all sorts of fashionably eccentric getups at the age of four. Frank was muse to my Coco.

Were your parents horrified?
Of course not, they loved it! Frank the transvestite teddy bear had the best wardrobe in the entire house.

Are you prone to mood swings?
No, very even-keeled. Never hurled a Giacometti sculpture . . .
yet.

Have you ever been mocked for any of your glamorous eccentricities?
I hope so. That means people are paying attention.

What is the most eccentrically glam thing in your closet?
My collection of vintage Ungaro dresses. They have lots of ruching so they make me feel as if I've been totally gift wrapped.

Have you ever wished you could trade in your life of glamorous eccentricity for one of dreary conformity?
Absolutely not! I'm addicted and loving it.

When does eccentric glamour become idiocy?
Never. It's fun to blur the lines between costume and what's fashionable.

Who is your inspirational icon of glamorous eccentricity?
Doris Duke and Iris Apfel. Of course, the Marchesa Casati pretty much invented the genre.

Do men think you are hot?
My husband does, and that's all that matters.

What is the thing that most offends your glamorously eccentric sensibilities?
Open-toe sandals with too long nails and a French pedicure with rhinestones. Eeeuw!

Where do you wish to be buried, and in what?
Whatever is in vogue in a hundred years. I hope there will be
some draping and ruching going on. I want to be gift wrapped
for eternity.

CHAPTER 10

A Large Woman
on a Small Stool

An etiquette for the twenty-first century

Good morning, class. Today I am going to teach you a vital and life-changing nugget of etiquette called the picture pose.

I stole it from an insanely magical old tome titled *The Berkeley School Guide to Beauty, Charm and Poise* published by Milady in 1962. The picture pose is on page 100. See that drawing of the chick standing in the doorway? She's practicing her picture pose.

Want to try? It's terribly easy. Run to the nearest doorway and go for it!

Place your left foot forward.
Place your left hand on your hip in a loose fist.
Place your right hand on the door frame, shoulder

157

high. Your fingers will point upward toward the ceiling.

Why, you may well ask, are you standing in the doorway as if breaking wind?

Read the text and all will be revealed.

> The self-conscious woman has a tendency to "sneak" into a room as though she had no right to be there. She furtively glances around, selects the first chair in sight and then rushes pell-mell, half-seated in the process, to become as obscure as possible. Her first impulse is to sit immediately.
>
> When a poised woman [that's supposed to be you] comes into a room through an open doorway, she pauses for a moment to orient herself.
>
> She will make mental notes, first of all, on the people in the room. They will be the focal point of her interest. Then she will look for a chair that will flatter her height and build. A large woman will look ridiculous on a small stool. A small girl, five foot two with eyes of blue, will be buried, quite literally in a wingback chair.

What possible function can this demented snippet of anachronistic etiquette serve you, the glamorous eccentric?

According to the good folks at Milady, the picture pose "allows others a moment to become aware of your presence."

Voilà!

The regular assumption of the picture pose is vital for those who are in the process of increasing their commitment to eccentric glamour. By pausing in the door frame you, the glamorous eccentric, are able, by observing your impact on colleagues and friends, to monitor the progress of your style metamorphosis.

The picture pose is shockingly easy to execute. A little practice makes perfect. Yes, I said practice.

The folks at the Berkeley School suggest that, before inflicting your picture pose (P.P.) on your friends and colleagues, you take a few moments to stand in the doorway at home and practice—repeatedly assuming and "dissolving" your P.P.—until you are picture-perfect. Do not stint on the practice runs. When you make your first foray into public picture posing, you do not want your fingers to be pointing the wrong way on the door frame.

I am a huge advocate of the picture pose. Applicable to both men and women, this miniritual is so profoundly useful that I feel it should be taught in schools. Incorporating the P.P. into your life must be undertaken with an air of devotional reverence. Picture posing is serious business. Picture posing can change the world.

Imagine how much more interesting, meaningful and—yes!—exciting life would be if, at every business meeting, high school prom, gallery opening, or family gathering, new arrivals would pause in the doorway, assuming "this beautiful asymmetrical pose."

Humdrum activities—taking out the garbage, entering a nail salon—would be treated with a newfound enthusiasm and respect by all parties concerned. By dignifying the day-to-day, we increase our appreciation for the simple things in life. It's positively Buddhist. Every poseur would enter every room with a heightened sense of his or her importance and its impact on others. There would be no more nose picking or crotch scratching. Instead of skulking into the room as if the gathering, and their attendance, was of no consequence, individuals would all rise to the occasion. Each arriving poseur would contribute to the general pool of glamour—eccentric and otherwise—thereby averting wars and other countless horrors.

Back in 1962, when the publishing house of Milady was cranking 'em out, etiquette, and the learning thereof, was part of a young lady's rite of passage. Every miss learned how to walk with a book on her head and how to pick a stool that matched the size of her ass. Etiquette was critical: Learning how to get out of a car without flashing your panties to the whole neighborhood—Britney *bonjour!*— was as important as breathing. Lapses in etiquette had fatal consequences: Sloppy girls who could not hold a knife and fork correctly were often thrown in the local loony bin or accused of being communists.

Ah! The good old days!

Unfortunately, the counterculture arrived and the concept of etiquette went out of style. Sixties flower children thought etiquette was "for squares, man." Any hippie who stood in the doorway of the yurt or local head shop practicing the picture pose would be ignored or assumed to be undergoing some kind of bad trip, man.

Eccentric Etiquette

It has been decades since the subject of etiquette was taken seriously. A twenty-first-century guide to mores and manners, in particular something that addresses the needs of the emerging glamorous eccentric, is sorely needed.

The glamorous eccentric is gregarious and curious. She is interested in all aspects of contemporary culture. She is mixing and mingling in a broad range of social milieux. The following etiquette is designed to make her journey enriching and more pleasurable.

Impertinent Questions

Formerly the opposite of good etiquette, asking blunt questions is now positively de rigueur.

Asking people's gender

As the transgender frenzy continues and cross-dressers and F-to-Ms proliferate, it is vital that we be permitted to ask complete strangers, glamorous eccentrics notwithstanding, "Are you a man or a woman?"

When young ladies—especially those attending the nation's more prestigious colleges—are growing sideburns and having double mastectomies, it is only reasonable that one should be able to confront this issue head on by asking, "Are you Arthur or Martha?"

I personally would welcome this revision to social etiquette. Being on the petit side, I am constantly being mistaken for a woman, especially if I wear a tightly belted trench coat and oversized dark glasses.

This, in and of itself, is not a problem. To have one's gender misidentified is not such a big deal. To be told that one is entering the wrong bathroom is mildly embarrassing and little more.

The *real* problem lies with the misidentifier.

If these people—taxi drivers, waitresses, and the like—mistakenly call me "madam" and I then take it upon myself to correct them, they are often far from pleased.

When I say, " No, sorry, luv, I am a bloke," they tend to

have one of two reactions, both of which I could live without.

More often than not, the stranger gets irate.

If I say, "Actually, it's 'sir' and not 'madam,' " the typical taxi driver tut-tuts and gives me a how-dare-you-make-a-fool-out-of-me-by-not-looking-more-gender-appropriate kind of a look. Blame the vic! Suddenly it's all *my* fault. Others' disappointment in their own perceptual abilities—"I'm so dumb, I cannot even tell what gender people are"—morphs into anger that is directed at me, the object of their misidentification, the innocent bystander.

The alternative reaction is, for me, no less perturbing. Those who do not become annoyed at me invariably prostrate themselves with contrition: "Oh. I am sosssoooo sorry!" they shriek as if misidentifying a man as a woman was a crime akin to slapping a grandmother.

This entire drama, with all its sexist implications, could be avoided if the interrogator had the carte blanche to establish gender in a straightforward manner.

Asking how much things cost

Long considered the height of nouveau riche vulgarity, asking the price of something is not only necessary, it's now a life-and-death matter. This applies not only to glamorous eccentrics but to the entire populace. Why? Because expensive things now look cheap and cheap things are now made to look expensive. This is especially true of handbags.

Asking a lady's age

Now that so many women—yes, I'm talking about those Evas again—have fake hair and fake boobs, and resemble thirty-something, bleach-blond prostitutes, it is vital that the glam eccentric be given carte blanche to break with the conventional notions of politesse. If someone is so Botoxed that you have absolutely no idea whether that someone was born before or after the war—the Crimean War, that is—it is extremely hard to engage in normal conversation.

Asking if a person has had work done

Now that women of all ages are going through the torture and expense of transforming themselves into thirty-something, bleach-blond prostitutes, it is only polite to show an interest in which particular procedures were undertaken to achieve this look.

(Following on the previous two pointers, it must now be socially acceptable to ask someone whether she is, in fact, a thirty-something, bleach-blond prostitute.)

Meeting and greeting without germs

I've ranted about the horrors of handshaking for years and nobody listened. The result? All kinds of plagues—mumps and bedbugs—are making a comeback.

In an effort to stay germ free, I have adopted, with great success, my own signature wave. I thoroughly recommend that everyone, regardless of how glamorous or eccentric, follow suit. A signature wave not only keeps the cooties at bay by eliminating all casual physical contact, it adds a memorable *je ne sais quoi* to your picture pose entrances.

Here's how I do mine: I hold my fist level with my shoulder, as if I am about to make a black power salute. I then flex my fingers up and down in tight unison. The look and feel of this wave recalls the gesturing paw of those large plaster cats that adorn untrendy Japanese restaurants.

Lolling and lounging—the new guest etiquette

A glamorous eccentric rarely stands for any length of time. She is what the French call *une grande horizontale.*

Despite the self-evident glamour of the lounging position, I find that people in general are reluctant to assume a recumbent position. When family or friends come to my house for dinner or cocktails, I have a terrible time getting them to sit down and recline.

In my mind's eye I see them all lounging on floor pillows, à la Yves Saint Laurent in Marrakech circa 1971. My guests rarely seem to share my vision: In a bizarre and incomprehensible gesture of politesse, the guests, no matter how bohemian or wacky, all stand in an erect cluster in the middle of the living room, looking like a choir of lost children.

Nothing I do, no amount of badgering, succeeds in getting them to sit.

I have tried various methods. I have even toyed with inducing physical collapse by grinding up quaaludes, or more up to date downers, into their drinks.

At my last gathering I tried the following ruse: I sidled up to a guest and hissed, "I just had this couch reupholstered. Would you mind trying it out and telling me if you think it's too poofy?" This worked for only a moment or two, before the guest popped up again.

The only thing that seems to work is to tell them exactly what I have in mind: "I am striving to evoke the ambience of a Parisian salon—you know, George Sand, Marcel Proust—so sit down before I strike you with this handy Lucite obelisk!"

Hostess gifts

Thanks to the easy hookups of the internet, the cost of dating has plummeted. The three candlelit dinners that were normally required before you could put your hand inside a person's blouse without seeming pushy are a thing of the past. The cost savings for daters have been so spectacular that a new etiquette seems in order.

When descending on a stranger's pad for a bit of what the Brits call "slap and tickle," it seems only fair to bring a host or hostess gift. There is nothing glam or eccentric about arriving empty-handed.

Since you do not know his or her décor style, it seems best to stick with food (e.g., chocolate-covered pretzels). If you are counting calories, there's always that old standby, the scented candle. Since other people's houses always smell bad, you may wish to light it before you enter: "Look what I brought you! Doesn't it smell fab? Now what was your name, again?"

Pot dealer etiquette

This is primarily aimed at all you Gypsies: Having your pot dealer drop by someone else's chichi art-world dinner party never failed to cause a shudder of horror and indignation among host and guest alike. As a nonsmoker—and therefore a Switzerland of sorts—I feel I can bring some neutrality and objectivity to this situation. Honesty compels me to admit that I am pro–pot dealer: The arrival of a mysterious and attractive criminal adds a memorable frisson of excitement to any occasion. Just don't try it at my house.

Shiny happy people

Instituting a new etiquette will not meet with much resistance. I suspect that most of your chums will welcome it. A spirit of cooperative gentility characterizes the times we live in. In my opinion, the general population has become much more polite than in the past. Surprising, isn't it? People may be piercing and tattooing every extremity and dressing like hos and pimps, but they are, in general, far more genteel than their boozy, belligerent grandparents.

There are those who disagree with me. Books about the deplorable state of contemporary manners are a dime a dozen. The assertion that our manners have degenerated is made, in my opinion, by people with lousy memories.

Examples:

- Road rage was much worse before there was a name for it.

- In the 1970s, everyone was getting raped and murdered. The only way to protect yourself was to become a big butch vigilante à la Charles Bronson.

- In the past, a trip to the movies—even *Bedknobs and Broomsticks*—invariably entailed sitting next to someone who chain-smoked unfiltered cigarettes. As a result, for most of my childhood I smelled like a kipper.

- In the past, people thought nothing of saying things like, "Hey, coolie! What time is it?" (When I first arrived in the United States in the 1970s, I heard this question hurled at a Chinese man from a passing car.)

- In the past, men pinched women's asses and perverts used to pinch my knees when I rode the bus in my little gray school shorts. To live was to be pinched.

If a whiny person—i.e., someone who did not get pinched as often as he or she might have preferred—wants to demonstrate how manners in our society have degenerated, that person usually focuses on some aspect of communications technology. Boring rants about cell phone usage are part and parcel of any conversation about contemporary social etiquette.

As someone who would much rather listen to other people's cell phone chats than to my own, I find the prevailing anti-phone attitude very twee and incomprehensible.

I am always fascinated and grateful to hear a complete stranger yakking loudly about her indigestion or making plans for the evening. To cell phone users, I say, "Don't be so selfish! Turn up the volume! Don't you have speaker phone?"

As a glamorous eccentric, it is vital that you have as much information as possible about other people's private lives. You are a student of human nature. What could be more fascinating and inspiring than these miniwindows into the lives and dramas of others?

Where is this cell phone user dining?

With whom?

What will these two lovers be eating?

Why aren't they more excited about it?

Are they really in love, or is this a breakup date?

They like brussels sprouts. Me too!

When the lady enters that particular restaurant to meet her beau, will she have the good sense to pause in the doorway to "allow others to become aware of her presence?" Will she find a stool that is the right size for her butt?

*"I've been mocked for wearing
exactly what the mockers wind up
wearing ten years later."*

AMY FINE COLLINS

Author, mother, Vanity Fair *scribe, muse to Geoffrey Beene and to Ralph Rucci, an egret of 1950s new look elegance responds to the Eccentric Glamour questionnaire.*

What are you wearing?

At this very moment I am wearing a moss-colored, sleeveless wool-jersey Ralph Rucci trapeze dress, with a crocodile insert under the bust. On my feet are Manolo zebra-linen sling-backs with mother-of-pearl paillettes.

When did you first realize that you might in fact be a glamorous eccentric?

When I asked my grandfather to polish the scuffed soles of my new Buster Brown black patent leather Mary Janes.

Were your parents horrified?

My parents were enablers.

Are you prone to mood swings?

If I get less than ten hours of sleep a night, yes.

Have you ever been mocked for any of your glamorous eccentricities?

I've been mocked for wearing exactly what the mockers wind up wearing ten years later. For example, at Columbia University in 1985, I was teased for wearing "bedroom slippers" to class. FYI: Those were the first Manolo mules seen in America. Around the same period a mother and child pointed and laughed at me for wearing Pucci. During the years I lived in the South—late '60s to early '70s—I was taunted for my mod minidresses and then for my haute hippie drag.

What is the most eccentrically glam thing in your closet?

The three-way mirror, in which I see my reflection!

Have you ever wished you could trade in your life of glamorous eccentricity for one of dreary conformity?

Sometimes I dream of reducing my wardrobe to a uniform of black trousers and black cashmere sweaters.

When does eccentric glamour become idiocy?

When you lose your social conscience, and desperate vanity overtakes you.

Who is your inspirational icon of glamorous eccentricity?

I have always been inspired by the drawings of Gruau and Eric.

Do men think you are hot?

What do you think? The men from whom I hear the most admiring comments are homeless, gay, black street people. Maybe that's because they feel they've got nothing to lose by speaking their minds. Any further information on this subject is too private or too dangerous to divulge!

What is the thing that most offends your glamourously eccentric sensibilities?

Conformity, naturally, and fear, which actually is the source of conformity. I have no respect for people with received ideas and received tastes who don't recognize them as such. I'm also impatient with people who adopt the form of things without understanding their substance.

Where do you wish to be buried, and in what?

It's hard to choose what to wear for the final exit, and this is why: I'd like to go out in the dress I had on during the happiest moments of my life. There is already a huge abundance of happy moments—and therefore too many dresses to choose from—and, as Frank Sinatra sings, "The best is yet to come." So how about this: Why not let my daughter choose what she wants to keep for herself, and then bury me pharoah-style with the rest of my wardrobe? There's already a plot for me at Woodlawn, but with this scenario probably not enough room.

CHAPTER 11

A-List Celebs
Don't Puke in Their Purses

Fame and the glam eccentric

Eccentric glamour, whether Existentialist, Gypsy, Socialite, or any combo thereof, will increase your visibility. The glamorous eccentric looms larger in her community or workplace than the average lady.

As your eccentric glamour quotient increases, so will your notoriety. People will remember you. People will drop their magazines when you enter the nail salon and say things like, "Thank God you're here! Now, tell me, where did you get that Gendarme cape and how did you figure out it would look so good with those Gap capri pants?"

A certain notoriety is part of the deal. Brace yourself for the increased attention.

People say fame is a bitch. I think it would be more accurate to say, "Fame is a bitch, but a dash of low-level notoriety is absolutely gorgeous!"

I come from a showbiz family: My great-aunt Florence was a ventriloquist. Let me rephrase that: My great-aunt Flo was a lousy amateur ventriloquist. "You can see her lips moving from across the street," people always said whenever Flo's name came up. Despite the shortcomings of her performances, Aunt Flo, a glam eccentric in a **splashy** print frock invariably accessorized with a doll of some description, enjoyed that genre notoriety of which I speak. Flo loomed large, albeit only within a ten-block radius of her humble row house. She was an F-list celebrity back when Kathy Griffin was just a mewling brat.

When the subject of fame comes up, I always think of long-deceased Great-Aunt Florence: Flo's level of fame is the best! Brad and Angelina and Madonna and TomKat should pray every night that their fame could become as dusty and iffy as Flo's. Flo has, in this regard, been a beacon of inspiration to myself. Thanks to this deceased ventroquilist I too am the proud possessor of an exquisitely second-rate notoriety. I am as famous as Flo, the well-liked but lousy ventriloquist: i.e., not very.

However, I would not trade my F-list fame for all the leg warmers in Jane Fonda's attic. While A-listers may get more freebies than me, the quality of my life is infinitely preferable to theirs.

Here's how I see it: If an A-lister tries to walk down Fifth Avenue, he or she will be mobbed and torn in two. He or she will end up seeking refuge in the American Girl store, or worse.

When, on the other hand, yours truly walks down Fifth Avenue, for about, say, twenty-five blocks or so, someone will, eventually, if I walk slowly enough, come up to me and say, "I saw you making fun of Gary Coleman on *I Love the 80's*. Were you wearing makeup?" or "I read your last column about butt bleaching and I think you should be locked up."

My fan base includes, I am happy to report, large numbers of African-American women. Having clocked me on *America's Next Top Model*, these Tyra Banks devotees take great pleasure in reclocking me. They whoop and holler and call me "girlfriend."

"You made that li'l gal cry," they crow, while wagging their fingers. "You are baaaad!"

Having been recognized, and often jiggled at, I am free to catch the bus home feeling all warm and fuzzy.

This low level of fame—it compares well with that of a small-town beauty queen—is so life-affirming that I now understand why old snaps of Flo show a broadly smiling eccentric. It wasn't just the clenched grin of a habitual ventriloquist. Flo was smiling because she was happy, happy to be ever so slightly famous.

Given how infinitely more pleasant my life is than theirs, I am surprised that successful people—I refer to those A-listers with the totally major wattage—are not begging and bribing people like me and Flo to help them achieve the same soggy notoriety. They should be saying things to me like, "I want you to help me reach that same tepid level of public recognition that you enjoy on a daily basis."

It's just as well that these A-listers are not seeking my help. I'm not sure I could help with their predicament. While Flo fame is easily within the grasp of the average glamorous eccentric, the same cannot be said for the average Hollywood A-lister. If you, Nicole Kidman, are reading this chapter, I send you my deepest sympathy on your situation. For you to become less famous—even to go from A-list to D-list—would be virtually impossible. If you suddenly start riding the bus or doing ordinary things like swapping recipes with neighbors, getting your hair done at Supercuts, chowing down at Sbarro, picking up your own dry cleaning or your doggie's poop, people will assume you are losing your marbles and you will receive even more unwanted attention than you do now, to mention nothing of the avalanche of rehab brochures that will pour through your letterbox every day.

You, dear glamorous Socialite, Existentialist, or Gypsy, are in an infinitely better position than the Lady Kidman. While Nicole's chances of reversing the process and achieving that gorgeously low level of semi-obscurity are zero, your chances of going from obscurity to a gorgeously low level semi-obscurity are actually quite good.

How I Did It

Real celebs are picky. They say no to everything and hire people to cherry-pick their press opportunities. The easiest way to join me on the F-list is to do the absolute screaming opposite. Say yes—emphatically, YES!—to everything.

I am living proof of the effectiveness of this approach. To imply that I have always been amenable and available to members of the press would be a ghastly, vile understatement. In fact, I have no recollection of ever, ever, ever turning down a request from a journalist.

In the pursuit of my Flo fame, I have been willingly interviewed for late-night Swedish radio stations. I have spewed aphorisms at the junior editors of obscure Chilean fashion quarterlies. I have helped fill the pages of Russian start-up magazines with quips about handbags. The only magazine on earth that I have yet to give a quote to is probably *Juggs*. (I hope someone from *Juggs* is reading this and will have the initiative to call.)

Having just turned down an opportunity for a podcast interview with an online Polish fashion website (in order to finish this book), I am stricken with guilt. I cannot shake the feeling that I have thrown away the opportunity of a lifetime, not to mention having turned my back on the good people of Poland. Overexposure schmoverexposure.

I do not, and cannot, and never will subscribe to the notion of overexposure.

I firmly believe that, as many appearances as a person can make on Welsh TV, there are new Welsh people being born every day who are desperate to hear snappy quotes about fashion and style and God knows what else. My philosophy has always been, "Leave no Welsh person unturned."

Royal Flush

As you claw your way from the bottom rung to the second from bottom rung, remember that fame can come via many avenues. It's not just about showbiz. Think laterally. Minor fame and notoriety need not necessarily come from a career as stand-up comedian, actress or, like Flo, a rotten ventriloquist.

There are many unexploited weird niche professions in which it is, paradoxically, much easier for the glamorous eccentric—or anyone else, for that matter—to make her mark. It is much easier to distinguish yourself in a dusty forgotten milieu than in a more high-profile and competitive one like pop music or fashion design.

Why not become the most famous eyebrow tweezer?

Or the waitress with the biggest beehive in the world?

You could be the world's only tap-dancing hotel concierge.

The world's most flamboyant construction worker.

The bank teller with the longest—or shortest— nails in history.

The slenderest postal worker.

I myself am probably the world's leading example of this phenomenon. I became, after years of slog, the world's most notorious window dresser. By putting edgy, disturbing things—stuffed rats, coffins, suicide depictions—into the shop windows of fancy luxury emporiums, I made a name for myself.

Window dressing is not the only thing I am slightly famous for. In addition to my window dressing notoriety, I am known for my impersonation of Her Majesty Queen Elizabeth II.

Don't smirk. Being a professional celebrity look-alike is not nearly as tawdry and pathetic as it sounds. (That would not be possible.) Believe me, I know what I'm talking about. Upon this subject, I am something of an expert. Having impersonated Queen Elizabeth II on no fewer than three occasions over the last thirty years—and been undercompensated to do so—I think I may claim to know whereof I speak.

Q. E. 1—The Launch

As I look back at my slightly spotty but otherwise long and happy celeb look-alike career, I am filled with a warm glow. A montage of images, mostly featuring me wearing a tiara and a sash, flits through my brain. Ah, I would not trade in those squishy memories for anything. And I certainly would not trade in being a look-alike for being the real thing. Why? Because to be the impersonator of a particular celebrity is much, much, much more fun than actually *being* that particular celebrity.

Think about it:

You can be Britney without ever having slept with Kevin Federline and lost your marbles.

You can be Michael Jackson without having to entertain all those annoying children.

You can be Marie Antoinette or Eleanor Roosevelt without being dead.

You can be Anna Nicole Smith without being dead or having been obliged to lap-dance an octogenarian.

Simply put, being a look-alike is infinitely less demanding and stressful than being the object of your impersonation. The expectations are so much lower. There is simply no comparison.

I realized this important fact on my first outing as Queen Liz.

On this particular occasion, Her Majesty was in an especially boisterous mood. With good reason. The year was 1981: Her son was marrying Diana on that very day. While the real queen was attending the dreary, endless nuptials in rainy England, I was living it up in Hollywood, California.

If my memory serves me correctly, the reigning monarch kicked off the evening with a heavy lard-infused Mexican combination platter at El Coyote, her favorite Mexican restaurant.

Keeping with the Mexican theme, she then proceeded to knock back about five large margaritas. The cost of these beverages was absorbed by Her Majesty's subjects, who seemed to take a perverse pleasure in watching H.M. get thoroughly smashed.

This was a lethal combination for a British stomach: Neither the queen nor I was up for the challenge. (Tip: It's nice to have something in common with your look-alike. It creates a sense of ownership while impersonating.)

Red faced and somewhat disheveled—and missing one of her long white gloves—the queen fell into the backseat of a friend's banged-up Camaro and headed to the official engagement of the evening: I was being paid $35—plus unlimited drink tickets—to cut the ribbon at a brand-new Hollywood nightclub.

During the short ride, the queen began to feel queasy. Her foundation garments, constricting her digestive tract as they were wont to do, were not helping matters. She thought she needed some air. She rolled down the window. Her nausea increased. Ere long, Her Majesty arrived at her destination. She hurriedly performed her official obligations to a blizzard of flashbulbs. She knew she was about to vomit, but in which direction? Even in her drunken state she knew that it would be decidedly unregal to blow chunks directly onto the splashy, vibrant new carpet with which this new establishment had seen fit to cover its floors. Her Maj took the only course of action available to her: she snapped open her large white purse and filled it with regurgitated enchiladas.

It was at this exact point that I realized how lucky I was *not* to be the actual queen. How on earth would she, Betty Windsor, have coped with the embarrassment of such an episode? How could she ever atone? There would be no way to reclaim her dignity. She would have been obliged to immolate herself in front of Buckingham Palace, waving the while.

And what of her subjects? It's impossible to imagine what the Brits would have made of the sight of the real queen puking into her purse. Nobody could argue that this would have anything other than a tremendously negative impact on her image and approval ratings.

And yet, as her look-alike, I faced no such PR crisis. Whereas her prestige would have plummeted, mine soared. As a look-alike I was—rightly or wrongly—not held to the same exacting standard of decorum. Nobody seemed to object to my purse puking. *Au contraire!* They cheered. Loudly.

Q.E. 2

Are there, you are probably asking, any downsides to being a look-alike? One or two.

The bookings are infrequent and the pay scale is disappointing. Real celebrities—the ones we look-alikes are imitating—unarguably make considerably more money than us.

Be that as it may, I always found that life as a look-alike was not without its occasional windfalls. In the fall of 1983 I upped my fees and was paid $50 to christen another new nightspot.

While this line of work may not have turned me into Donald Trump (FYI, he's an easy look-alike to pull off and his popularity at the time of writing would definitely yield more bookings than my chosen look-alike ever did), it has availed me a great deal of wisdom. Being a celebrity look-alike has rendered me a sage of sorts.

My career as a look-alike has given me an in-depth understanding of, among other things, the power of celebrity, even faux celebrity.

Example: After fulfilling the $50 above-mentioned engagement, I was obliged to drive from the bowels of Hollywood to downtown L.A., in full queen drag.

Driving a pickup truck through graffiti-plastered neighborhoods while dressed as Her Maj was not without its frisson of surrealism.

As chance would have it, my route took me through some really dodgy neighborhoods, including the MacArthur Park area. I looked upon this as an educative opportunity for the queen: "This, Your Royal Highness, is where the paupers live. As you will see, they have no corgis."

At a stoplight on Pico Boulevard, a carload of Chicano gang members pulled up alongside me. Their flame-colored vehicle bounced and gurgled. Wild *pachanga* music blared from the interior.

In an unguarded moment I glanced over and caught the eye of a stylish young man in a hairnet. He had a tattooed teardrop below his left eye. On spotting Her Maj, the swarthy lothario began to yell incomprehensible things in Spanish. I caught the words *pendeja* and *maricón*.

Doing my best to keep my sangfroid, I raised a gloved hand and waved à la Betty Windsor. This gesture had an immediate and powerful effect. The young men in the adjacent vehicle did not appear to understand the benign nature of this piece of legendary hand choreography. Assuming I was trying to start a turf war, the swarthy lads erupted out of their vehicle. They surrounded my truck and began to gesture right back at me, throwing gang signs left and right. My white court shoe floored the accelerator and I tore off into the night.

Q.E. 3

To this very day, my career as a celebrity look-alike continues to teach me valuable life lessons.

In the spring of 2001, Barneys, my employer, unveiled a small Co-op boutique on Wooster Street. The budget for the opening party was limited. There was not the requisite cash to throw a celeb red-carpet bash. Look-alikes were the most obvious alternative.

In a cavalier moment I told the top brass at Barneys that I would find someone to impersonate Queen Elizabeth II to add sizzle to the ribbon cutting. Having been one myself, I rashly assumed that queen look-alikes were a dime a dozen.

A call was placed to a look-alike agency. I requested a Liza, a Marilyn, a Michael Jackson, and a Q.E. 2.

The agency called back to say that, though they had a queen, she had just undergone a medical procedure and was resting at her daughter's apartment in Secaucus, New Jersey. I panicked and begged. She would not budge. No amount of cash would induce her to don her tiara. As a consolation prize the agency offered me something special: a Wolf Blitzer.

An *Abfab*-ian panic now filled the Barneys PR office. The die was cast. A press release had already gone out indicating the arrival of Her Majesty. We simply had to find a queen.

Word somehow leaked out about my former look-alike career, and before you could say "butt pads," a professional stylist, hairdresser, and makeup artist arrived *chez moi* and I was being corseted and painted like a circus grotesque.

It felt good to be, as it were, back in the saddle, especially as I did not have to do all the painstaking prep myself.

After three hours I was looking pretty damn regal. I took stock in the mirror and surveyed my middle-aged visage. Her Majesty and I had been through a lot together.

After a light snack—no Tex-Mex—I mentally prepared myself to leave my apartment *en femme*. This was the first time I had "done" the queen in broad daylight. I was used to what we look-alikes call "cover of darkness."

After navigating the obliviousness of my doorman—for details of this encounter I refer you back to the introduction—I climbed into the bicycle rickshaw that would convey me through the streets of lower Manhattan to the ribbon-cutting ceremony. I felt strangely elated. My doorman's magnificent indifference had proved something important to me, something that every glamorous eccentric should keep in mind as she goes about her transformation.

It proved to me the utter pointlessness of ever being self-conscious about anything. You can worry obsessively about what people think of you and your appearance. You fret. You feel like you are being horribly judged twenty-four hours a day. You gnash your teeth. You try to second-guess the world. You imagine all sorts of awful commentary about your ratty hair or you tragic outfits as soon as your back is turned.

But all these concerns are a total waste of time, *because nobody cares!*

You can leave your apartment with a peacock feather sticking out of your bottom and your doorman's only comment will be, "There's a package here for you. Do you want it now or later?"

As you experiment with your appearance, you must remember that by feeling self-conscious you are merely indulging yourself. Nobody is judging you. You are free! You could set fire to yourself in front of Macy's and nobody would bat an eye. People are much too busy worrying about their own lives to ask why you are dressed up as Wolf Blitzer.

Lest I have painted too rosy a picture of the life of a celebrity look-alike, let me acknowledge a downside or two. While real queens have the world at their feet, and everyone hangs on their every word, the same cannot be said for we look-alikes. We are expected to be—yawn!—flexible. This was brought home to me in no uncertain terms on that last outing.

As we rounded the corner into Wooster Street, I instructed my rickshaw chauffeur to stop in the middle of the block. I gave him these instructions in an authoritative, regal Catherine Zeta-Jones kind of way.

I leaned out of the vehicle and looked up ahead. A surprisingly large cheering crowd and a red carpet awaited me. As we approached, I got into character and prepared to meet my public.

Despite my clear-throated instructions, the young man kept right on pedaling. He continued to whiz south, past my adoring subjects, in the direction of Canal Street.

At this point I am ashamed to say that Her Majesty resorted to sarcasm.

"Okay, Marco Polo, turn this puppy around, and this time *stop* at the red carpet."

"Oh, was that for you?"

"Duh!"

When he kept right on pedaling, Her Majesty began whacking him with her purse.

"Sorry, lady, but this is a one-way street. I have to go back up Greene and come back down Wooster."

Fearing that, by the time this lengthy maneuver was accomplished, my subjects would have gotten bored and gone home, I jumped out and schlepped back up Wooster Street on foot. As much as the real Her Majesty loves a bracing constitutional in a tweed skirt, it's hard to imagine her dealing with this situation with the same uncomplaining accommodation.

The last and most important thing I learned about fame and celebrity during my career as a celebrity look-alike concerns bumpy roads, SoHo in particular.

When a rickshaw hurtles over cobblestones, it produces an intense series of vibrations. Under the right conditions, these vibrations can be sufficient to dislodge a tiara, giving the wearer the appearance of one who has enjoyed several glasses of sherry.

The following Sunday there was an intriguing photo of *moi*, tiara askew, in the *New York Times* cutting the red ribbon with a giant pair of scissors.

"Flo would be proud," I mused as I stuck the image in my scrapbook, hopefully to be found in a dusty attic by some fame-crazed spotlight-grabber in the future.

*"In Florence, Italy, recently,
an old lady called me a clown,
and not in a nice way."*

LYNN YAEGER

Village Voice *fashion editor, New York fashion fixture, devotee of rouge, Goyard bags, and Belgian avant-garde designers responds to the Eccentric Glamour questionnaire.*

What are you wearing?

A short black Comme des Garçons skirt over a huge white tutu from the Zara store in Barcelona with a thrift shop cardigan, a pair of slippers from discountdance.com, Wolford tights, and a lot of antique jewelry.

When did you first realize that you might in fact be a glamorous eccentric?

When I was in the third grade and refused to wear pants (and have never worn them again) and begged Mommy to buy me poufy "angel" blouses.

Were your parents horrified?

No, they were quite nice about it. Once when I was on fashion

TV and a friend of my mother's commented to her that they had made me up funny for the broadcast and my mom replied, "Oh, no! That's my Lynnie!"

Are you prone to mood swings?
You mean sartorially? I'm actually pretty consistent, clothing-wise and otherwise.

Have you ever been mocked for any of your glamorous eccentricities?
Well, growing up in Massapequa Park and wearing nutty clothes was no picnic basket, I can assure you. And they don't seem to like me all that much in France. Oh, and in Florence, Italy, recently, an old lady called me a clown, and not in a nice way.

What is the most eccentrically glam thing in your closet?
An old scarlet Romeo Gigli jacket covered with velvet petals that makes me look like a large (chic!) walking vegetable.

Have you ever wished you could trade in your life of glamorous eccentricity for one of dreary conformity?
No! But I do have a secret dread of having to go on a normal job interview one day.

When does eccentric glamour become idiocy?
Never.

Who is your inspirational icon of glamorous eccentricity?
I'm a big fan of Kiki de Montparnasse.

Do men think you are hot?
Oscar Wilde and Max Beerbohm both find me devastatingly attractive.

What is the thing that most offends your glamorously eccentric sensibilities?
Jeans. T-shirts. Sneakers. (Unless worn in an extremely cute way.)

Where do you wish to be buried, and in what?
Père-Lachaise, but not sure if being Jewish is a problem. And I hope this will be so far in the future, I haven't yet bought what I'll be wearing.

CHAPTER 12

Hurl Your Arms
Heavenward

A glam eccentric guide to weight loss

Eccentric glamour is an inclusive nonlooksist movement. All shapes and sizes are welcome.

It would, however, be thoroughly disingenuous—cruel, even!—not to address the sensitive issue of weight loss at some point in this book. As with other topics, I will commence exploration of this particular aspect of eccentric glamour with a related anecdote from my past. This yarn spotlights, among other things, the creativity displayed by a certain Oscar-winning glamorous eccentric in the arena of weight loss.

The Fear of Squat

Los Angeles, 1984.

She walked toward me wearing pink squishy Reeboks, white

leg warmers, and a shiny apricot bodysuit with a thong back. Her legs were encased in tan, slightly shimmery panty hose. As a result they looked as if they were made of plastic. Her accessories included a beige nylon LeSportsac fanny pack and a white terry cloth Olivia-Newton-John-Let's-Get-Physical headband with matching wristbands. She looked like a Patrick Nagel drawing come to life.

As she approached, I recognized this Lycra-clad lass: We were colleagues. She was a salesgirl at the same clothing store where I was dressing windows. A fashion elitist with a high eccentric glamour quotient, she was normally head to toe in the latest trendy imported garments. As a salesperson she was allowed to borrow the expensive clothes from the racks, returning them at the end of the day. As a lowly display person I enjoyed no such privileges: I, in my thrift-shop vintage *trouvées*, was left to covet the high-priced offerings.

She sprinted proudly down the beverage aisle in her otherworldly getup.

"Nifty outfit," I said, little knowing that within a matter of days I would be sucked into her cult and forced to wear almost exactly the same thing.

"Aerobics. You would love it," she said, deliberately reaching down to the lowest shelf for a vat of Evian water so that she could simultaneously stretch out her hamstrings and lower back. She popped up, leveled her gaze at me, and continued proselytizing, warming up her ankles the while.

"It's totally amazing. Aerobicizing burns so many calories, why, I can eat and drink as much as I want and *I'll never get fat!*"

She spat out the words. They fell to the linoleum supermarket floor and lay there like a glistening, challenging, irresistible gauntlet.

Never get fat. Never get fat. Never get fat. Never get fat.
This phrase reverberated in my conscious and unconscious minds. The idea of never getting fat held an enormous appeal for me. As a short person—my passport generously allows me five foot four and one half inches—I have lived with a crushing obligation to stay trim and slim. My mother Betty, a well-toned leprechaun if ever there was one, had instilled this obsession in me.

"Tall people can put on a few pounds and nobody will notice," Mrs. Doonan would opine, adding, "but if *we* put on weight, *we* end up looking *squat.*" And, thanks to cigarette smoking, riding a bicycle to work, and a long-line girdle, she never did.

When my mother went on these rants, I knew she was not using the royal "we." I knew she meant "we" as in me and her.

There was no point in contesting her hypothesis. She was so obviously correct: short + fat = squat. And there was nothing in the world worse than being *squat.* Everyone knew that. Everything that was desirable in life was slender and elongated. Squat things—toads, trolls, potbellied pigs, evil gnomes—were the very essence of undesirability. It was better to be criminally insane than end up *squat.*

On the advice of my coworker, I joined the Sports Connection.* For my debut class I cobbled together an outfit consisting of an old paint-spattered T-shirt, vintage checkered resort shorts, and a pair of oily baseball sneakers.

The allotted hour arrived. A sea of mostly female devotees in leotards and leg warmers began funneling up the stairs to the massive exercise studio overlooking Santa Monica Boulevard. My co–calorie burners all looked like Jamie Lee Curtis. Nobody was squat.

---

* Sports Connection: Location of the quintessential '80s aerobics movie *Perfect.*

The floor of the large studio was covered in mauve carpet. The walls were mirrored. In the space of about one minute the entire room filled up with stretching, gossiping aerobicizers. It was a star-studded group: I spotted Denise Crosby, Bing's granddaughter and soon to be star of *Pet Sematary*, and Dr. Toni Grant, the busty radio psychologist who dated pornographer Al Goldstein, who was not present but should have been since he tends toward squatness.

We positioned ourselves around the room in regimental rows. It was all very Leni Riefenstahl: The impeccably spaced, impeccably sculpted bodies reflecting into infinity gave the occasion the feeling of a Nuremburg rally, sponsored by Danskin.

The teacher, a feisty chick called Renee, slotted in her cassette tape. The disco version of "Memories" from *Cats* filled the air and the room exploded into unified movement.

To my surprise, I followed the movements of the teacher and the people around me quite effortlessly. Not only did I find the whole thing incredibly easy, I was actually good at it. I did not fall over once. The low center of gravity that put me at such extreme risk for squatness in the outside world was, here on the mauve carpet, a very distinct advantage.

By the time we began doing pull-downs, the most archetypal movement in the aerobics canon, I was totally in the swing of things. What a feeling! In a lifetime filled with bubbly vivacity, I had never felt like this before. I was literally ecstatic.

The pull-downs triggered a surge of endorphins, sending me into a state of borderline insanity. Shocking though it now sounds, I remember thinking, "This is my destiny." I had found some kind of spiritual home, a place where I could leap and squeal, and where squat-avoidance was guaranteed. I had gone temporarily insane.

The next day I was back, this time wearing a cheapo exercise outfit—black short shorts, turquoise muscle shirt, and snow-white scrunch socks—which my colleague picked out for me in the gym store. She suggested that I might care to incinerate my shabby début ensemble.

My new outfit was a big hit on the mauve carpet. Over the next few weeks I bought lots more. When you are aerobicizing every day, and twice on Saturdays, you need an infinite number of tights, crop tops, scrunch socks, jock straps, and dance belts.

My roommate at the time was that plain-speaking bloke called Robert who catapulted me in to sobriety in Chapter 8. He was bewildered and vaguely disgusted by my new enthusiasm. His idea of exercise was vacuuming while singing along to Laura Branigan's "Self Control": "City light—*vrooooom*— painted girl—*vrrooom!*"

This regimen seemed to work fine for him. He was tall and slender and had lovely long legs that he likened to those of hot-at-the-time model Jerry Hall, "except my ankles are better than hers." I envied his lissome frame: He would never know what it was like to live with the fear of becoming squat.

As my enthusiasm increased, so did Robert's disdain.

"My God! What's happened to you? It's like living with an overworked stripper!" he would complain, moving my rack of freshly rinsed skimpy garments out of the tub so that he could take a shower.

On occasion he would, using pastry tongs, grab one of the offending articles and demand an explanation.

"Which bits of you, pray tell, is this supposed to support?"

When I hit upon the idea of changing at home and jogging to class, Robert became even more vigilant: He insisted on inspecting me before I left the house.

"Not the leopard! It's much too nelly. You can't be skipping down Santa Monica Boulevard dressed like Cher," he would say disapprovingly. "Someone will shoot you from a passing car."

"Must rush. I want to get a good spot."

"What would your mother say if she knew you were flaunting yourself in public dressed like that?"

"As long as I didn't get squat," I said, rebelliously twanging my Norma Kamali tights into place—yes, I had graduated to tights— and tucking my front door key into one of my scrunch socks, "she would not care."

As the months flew by, I got progressively more addicted and became, as far as my frame would allow, the opposite of squat. I was high as a kite on my own endorphins, and I had never been thinner and more wiry in my entire life.

I got to know several of my fellow addicts. Since everybody tended to gravitate toward the same spot in each class, making friends with adjacent devotees was inevitable.

I frequently ended up next to a severe six-foot-tall blond Existentialist who drove a pink Cadillac convertible with furry dice and crucifixes hanging from the rearview mirror. We would lie parallel on that smelly, sweat-drenched carpet and do our leg exercises in unison while chatting. She told me she was a gossip columnist for the *National Enquirer*.

"Let me know if you see anything unusual," she said one day, during her flex 'n' points.

"Like what?"

"Oh, you know, movie stars acting weird. Joan Collins in a snit. A game show host feeling someone up. Stuff like that."

"Here?"

"Not necessarily. Maybe they're drunk in a restaurant. Farrah? Ryan? Morgan Fairchild? Surely you must have some dirt. Burt Reynolds? Linda Evans?"

"I just saw Dick Van Dyke at the supermarket."

"Was he red in the face? Was he buying liquor?"

"I did not look in his cart."

"See, this is what I mean! You've got to be more focused and much more observant."

Suddenly I felt as if *I* were working for the *National Enquirer.*

I might just as well have been. Every time I subsequently saw this girl, she would challenge me with a brusque, "Got any dirt?"

When I told her no, I felt like an underperforming employee, or a disappointing child who always came home with lousy grades. Then she would shake her head, sigh, and roll over to continue her leg lifts . . . one . . . two . . . three . . . four . . .

One day I was up a ladder changing a display. The new fall designer merchandise had arrived and the store was abuzz with extremely unsquat Hollywood types whose favorite pastime seemed to be shopping. This is in those long-lost halcyon days before celebs figured out they could get everything for free.

Suddenly the brouhaha got louder.

"Oh, my God! Shelley Winters," hissed a sales associate while jiggling my ladder and me.

It was true. The great Shelley Winters, the unconventional, taboo-busting winner of two Academy Awards, had entered the store. Within minutes she had galvanized the entire place with her charm and sassiness. She then proceeded to make one of the most unusual transactions I have ever witnessed. Atop my ladder, I had a bird's-eye view.

*   *   *

That night, on the mauve carpet, my gossip columnist friend sidled up to me with the usual question. "Got any dirt?"

"Not really. But I did see Shelley Winters buying a size six pair of leather pants."

Suddenly I had her full attention. She stopped midcrunch.

"Size six? Fantastic! And?"

The gossip columnist pulled out a tiny pad and pencil, which she kept in her fanny pack. She regarded me warmly. I felt as if I had finally brought home the bacon. I was no longer that loser who never had any Hollywood gossip.

"They were Gianni Versace, red-brown and—"

"She's not a size six. How the hell is she going to fit into—

"She said she wasn't going to wear them. She was going to hang them on her refrigerator door."

The muckraker gasped. She then made me repeat the story while she scribbled frantically. All this was accomplished while we flawlessly executed our remaining leg lifts.

Back home, I plopped my sweaty stripper gear into the sink and began to rinse. As the endorphin rush subsided, I started to feel increasingly creepy about what I had done. I shared the story with Robert.

"Relax!" said my platonic roommate reassuringly. "Just because you blabbed to the *National Enquirer* doesn't mean they can revoke your green card. Or does it?"

I had no idea how my employer would react if he ever found out: The celebrity clientele was the bread and butter of this particular store. I began to feel as if I had betrayed not only my boss—the sponsorer of said green card—but also the great Shelley herself.

How could I have done such a cheesy thing, ratting out a Hollywood great? And I was such a fan. I had seen every one of her movies.

I thought of Shelley's pathos-drenched performance in *A Place in the Sun*, in particular the moment when she finally puts two and two together and asks Montgomery Clift, "George? When you wish upon a star, do you wish that I was dead?"

Robert Mitchum had slit her throat in *Night of the Hunter*. James Mason had broken her heart, raped her daughter, and indirectly caused her death in *Lolita*. The Nazis had dragged her off to a concentration camp in *The Diary of Anne Frank*. Now it was my turn.

To make matters worse, I had betrayed Shelley at her most vulnerable, in her battle against squatness.

The following week my tidbit appeared in the *National Enquirer*, and my Shelley guilt returned full force. I toyed with driving around West Hollywood buying up all the copies.

A week later, just when my guilt was subsiding, I received a $50 check from the *National Enquirer* made out to me, "for Shelley Winters item."

At first I vowed not to cash the check. I would stuff it in an envelope. Then I decided to give it to charity. But which charity? How about calling Miss Winters's assistant to ascertain "the charity of Shelley's choice." Maybe that wasn't such a great idea. I shoved it in a drawer. How would I ever find a way to forgive myself?

The next day, a delivery of nifty fluorescent-hued Lycra items arrived at the store from the design house of Stephen Sprouse in New York. Designer aerobicswear! I grab a pair of cycle shorts—orange, black, and white with the signature Sprouse mirror writing and looked at the price tag. $50.

Time is a great healer. Within seconds I was healed.

I suddenly realized that Shelley's weight-loss trick—an anti-snacking device attached directly to the front of the refrigerator—was a uniquely creative squat-battling tip and one that I had, albeit unwittingly, now been instrumental in passing on to a wider audience. I had not betrayed Shelley. I had, if anything, aided her and the women of America in their battle against squatness. We were all foot soldiers in the same battle of the bulge. Maybe I should get a medal of some kind. Who knows how many weight watchers I might have helped.

Shelley would have been proud, or maybe she wouldn't have given a toss. Either way, in my nifty Sprouse cycle shorts, I was the talk of my aerobics class that night.

Tips for Glamorous Hips

What on earth, you may well ask, is the moral of this story? And what possible connection does it have to eccentric glamour?

As I see it, there is nothing wrong with squat avoidance. The glamorous eccentric is conscious of her body and will always strive to maintain a healthy flattering weight. The key is to do it with a bit of creative panache. Have fun with it. Accept your fear of squatness and combat it with some of that creativity which is part of the glamorous eccentric's modus operandi. Find an idiosyncratic way to shed those pounds.

The fact that Shelley Winters had such an ingenious weight-loss tip should not come as a huge surprise. All celebs are obsessed with the size of their bottoms, and justifiably so. The livelihood of these folks depends on their ability to either develop an eating disorder or maintain some kind of antisquat regimen.

To add to the pressure, celebs, more than those in any other profession, are horribly and poignantly prone to weight gain. The reason is simple: If you are a movie actor, you tend to make your money in large glistening dollops. You work intermittently. A dollop comes in, then you lollygag about waiting, and praying, for the next script. This puts you at severe risk for squatness. People who lie around the house all day in Malibu invariably start smoking marijuana. And, because celebs have loads of glistening cash on hand, this invariably turns into an astounding amount of marijuana. And people who smoke an astounding amount of marijuana and have gobs of money are quite likely to buy, and consume, in addition to the aforementioned marijuana, an astounding amount of Hostess Twinkies.

In warm climates, most food items, even ones containing an astounding amount of preservatives like Hostess Twinkies, are kept in the refrigerator. It comes as no surprise, therefore, that the Shelley technique—a warning talisman on the refrigerator door—was invented on the West Coast.

Maintaining a healthy weight is about finding the method—no matter how idiosyncratic—that is right for you. Before you follow Shelley's lead and rush out and buy a pair of leather pants, please know that there are many other equally eccentric and potentially effective options available to you.

The Barbi Benton Method

Miss Benton, ex-bunny and former star of *Hee-Haw*, offers a great variation on the Shelley Winters method. She installed mirrored panels on the fronts of all the refrigerators in her Aspen home. By confronting herself, midlunge, with her own reflection, Barbi gives herself that critical opportunity to decide whether she "really needs that snack." Her trim figure, and all those who admire it, are the happy beneficiaries of this brilliant strategy.

Warning: Unless you have a big staff of Windex-wielding, obsessive-compulsive maids, the mirrors will quickly become a finger-marked horror. My own preference is to bag the mirrors and simply to hang something on the fridge door that I find repulsive, unappetizing, or otherwise cautionary.

Like so many challenges in life, this is a fantastic opportunity for creativity and self-expression. Why not découpage the door with a montage of those tabloid celeb/cellulite snaps? Finding something that revolts is just as much fun as finding something that delights: How about a Thomas Kinkade painting? A photo from *National Geographic* of maggots eating a wildebeest carcass? *Bon appetit!*

The Muriel Spark Method

Dame Muriel Spark, a glamorously eccentric deceased British writer, often included chilling weight-loss themes in her writings. In *The Girls of Slender Means*, the thin girl survives, while the fat girl, unable to escape through the tiny bathroom window of the burning building, does not.

A specific weight-loss solution is offered in Spark's *A Far Cry from Kensington*. The main character, a chunky young war widow named Mrs. Hawkins, goes from stout to slender by meticulously eating half the food that is presented to her. Half the carrots, half the pudding, etc. She eventually becomes half her original size.

Those of you who opt for this technique can avoid appearing wasteful by enlisting the participation of another weight loser. She can dine on your discards.

The Zsa Zsa Gabor Method

As was seen so clearly in my aerobics odyssey, the pre-lipo '80s was a time when people tried to battle squatness the old-fashioned way, by exercising. When we weren't leaping around in leotards at the gym, we were doing the same thing at home, guided by one celebrity workout tape or another.

Celebrity workout tapes were a huge part of the Reagan era. Who knows what craven, zeitgeisty impulse caused this lemminglike rush toward the video camera—but rush they did: Heather Locklear, Joan Collins, Donna Mills, it really is hard to find a glamorous '80s star who was not willing to lie on her back, open her legs, and make a beauty or exercise video. If you have never viewed one of these cinematic masterpieces, you are in for a big treat. Those Jane Fonda tapes were really just the tip of the iceberg.

For the average glamorous eccentric like you, dear reader, these workout tapes are the perfect weight-loss aid. The combination of earnest idiocy and unconscious high camp appeals directly to your sophisticated sense of humor. Even if you never do the exercises, you will simply laugh away the calories. Whether it's Paula Abdul's *Cardio Dance* or Tanya Tucker's *Country Workout*, you're always guaranteed some thigh-slappin', calorie-burnin' fun.

It's the "unscripted" chitchat that provides the bulk of the chuckles. Examples:

Donna Mills in *The Eyes Have It*: "I wanna show you how to look pretty, whether you're outdoors or in a business situation."

General Hospital star Jackie Zeman in *Beauty on the Go*: "I think it's possible to meet all your obligations and still look and feel terrific."

My favorite is a 1994 tape called *It's Simple, Darling* by Zsa Zsa Gabor.

If, like me, you would rather work out alongside people who are less proficient than yourself—possibly an older Hungarian lady—then this is the tape for you. The busty, heavily accented, cop-slapping coquette meanders halfheartedly through an exercise routine so undemanding that it looks as if it would actually cause her to put on weight. It is the perfect tape for those who are easily demotivated by athletic prowess in others. There is no way on earth that, even if you had all your limbs amputated, you are not going to be more zippy than Zsa Zsa.

At the end of the day, it's not about the exercise, it's about the repartee. The typical Gabor banter about husbands and rings—"Ven you break your engagement, you must give beck ze ring . . . but keep ze stone"—is the gasoline that powers this curious enterprise.

Regarding her sixth husband: "I bought him a vaterbed to lighten zings up a bit . . . It vas a Dead Sea!"

Regarding Conrad Hilton: "Ven ve got divorced, he vas generous—he geff me five million Gideon Bibles . . . but I ztill like him. As a matter of fect, I still have hiz name on my tovels."

It's Simple, Darling, along with any of the above-mentioned classics, can be found by trawling endlessly on eBay, a calorie-burning exercise in itself.

The Mariah Carey Technique

This unique method works only for gals up to a certain weight. If you, like Mariah, vacillate between "voluptuous" and "zaftigish"—a ten-pound differential—it will work for you.

Caution: This two-pronged technique does not help you actually lose weight. It merely gives you the appearance of having shed a few pounds.

Prong one: Always wear high heels, arch your back a lot, and hurl your arms heavenward at the least provocation.

Prong two: Take your own paparazzi with you everywhere and edit the shots yourself.

The Totie Fields Technique

Back in the 1970s there was much discussion about what constituted a weight problem. It took the great borscht belt comedian and food advocate Totie Fields to clarify things for a confused nation.

According to Totie, you need to go on a diet if "Ralph Nader insists you rotate your shoes every four-thousand miles." Another telltale sign: If you wear white to a party and "the host shows movies on you," it may be time to think about weight loss.

Fat and dieting were central topics for Totie and her audience: "I went on a crash diet for two weeks and all I lost was fourteen days," she famously shrieked, creating waves of empathy with her be-girdled fans.

The sexual revolution impacted everything in the 1970s, including the world of dieting, but Totie was quick to pooh-pooh any misinformation about the relationship between copulation and calorie burning: "Having sexual relations only burns up one hundred and twenty calories, so it hardly seems worth it."

Totie's status as the patron saint of struggling dieters was confirmed after she pointed out that "the first three letters in the word 'diet' are 'die' " and that there were millions of Americans "who felt like doing just that, because they were on one."

Fueled by diet disillusion, in 1972 Totie penned the ultimate nose-thumber to the growing obsession with weight loss. It's called *I Think I'll Start on Monday*. It was written for all the pastry-lovin' broads whose "heartbeat quickens at the sight of an éclair or a hot-fudge sundae."

Why, you may well ask, am I advocating a reckless attitude to diet? How can such a truculent, uncooperative posture possibly help you lose weight?

Here's how: By chuckling about the whole subject and by not descending into a spiral of defeated misery, you will automatically fare better than the lady who does. Those who are riddled with insecurity and self-loathing will always make more trips to the refrigerator, and no amount of repellant imagery or leather pants will keep them out.

If you are unable to keep off the pounds and squatness prevails, do not despair. Totie to the rescue. She maintained an arsenal of incredibly useful ripostes for that moment when construction workers hurl an uncomplimentary remark or two regarding your less-than-svelte physique.

Here are a couple of classic Fields comebacks:

"I'm not fat. I just retain flesh."

"I'm not fat. I'm pregnant and I never gave birth. My baby just decided to live in."

Though I thoroughly applaud and highly recommend Totie's commitment to food and her cavalier attitude toward dieting, I would be doing you a disservice if I failed to point out that, a mere six years after writing *I think I'll Start on Monday*, the laughter abruptly stopped when Totie, whose real name was Sophie Feldman, succumbed to a diabetes-related illness.

The Maria Callas Technique

Legend has it that Maria Callas—one of the greatest chubby-to-fabulous icons of the last century—achieved her weight-loss goals by swallowing a tapeworm.

I dispute this notion: In my opinion she did it with eyeliner.

One day, while experimenting with her theatrical maquillage, her elbow must have slipped and she wooshed a line from the corner of her eye out across her eyelid. She did not stop. The brush kept on going. By the time she had finished she had drawn a long line almost to her hairline. She replicated the line above the other eye and—bingo!—she created her catlike signature look.

This new, unplanned makeup trick was utterly transformative. She had found that signature gesture which was to make her one of history's greatest glamorous eccentrics. She took one look at herself and realized that something major had happened: She was no longer the tubby gal from Athens with the fabulous voice and the dimply arms. A vision of a unique beauty revealed itself.

Hold the baklava!

The diva then dieted her way to stardom. With two wicked swipes of the eyeliner brush, La Callas became the style icon with the couture wardrobe.

I cannot guarantee that the same thing will happen to you, but given the low cost involved—two dollops of eyeliner!—it may be worth a try.

The Andy Warhol Technique

Back in the 1970s, Warhol, my muse and the twentieth century's most inspiring artist, developed a taste for chocolate. Teuscher was apparently his favorite. Terrified of getting fat, he developed a kind of functional bulimia: He would chew them briefly and spit the result into a paper towel.

(A note for those who adopt this method: Spitting out every chocolate seems a bit wasteful, especially with an expensive brand like Teuscher. How about every other choccie?)

Andy had another and possibly more useful tip: He called it the Andy Warhol New York City Diet. He explained it as follows: "When I order in a restaurant, I order everything I don't want, so I have a lot to play around with while everyone else eats. Then, no matter how chic the restaurant is, I insist that the waiter wrap the entire plate up like a to-go order."

Andy would then leave the gourmet offerings for the delectation of a random homeless person who will happily find "a Grenouille dinner on the window ledge."

Love Yourself Like Karl

"I don't like skinny people. I think it's very démodé."
—*Karl Lagerfeld*, 1977, after chunking up a tad

"Muscles are out. Bones are in."
—*Karl Lagerfeld*, 2002,
thirty-five years later,
after shedding ninety pounds

Busted!

Karl Lagerfeld's dramatic weight loss—in 2005 he published a book about it called *The Karl Lagerfeld Diet!*—has been a hot topic in the world of fashion for much of the early twenty-first century, which doesn't say much about la mode's ability to generate hot topics. Be that as it may, the riveting-ish details of the Chanel designer's corn bread 'n' veggie diet—not to mention his subsequent penchant for high-waisted women's jeans—have clogged the fashion press for so long now that a whole generation of people has come along who no longer remember cookie-jar Karl.

Imagine my glee when I happened upon his earlier, fat-positive declarations in which Herr Lagerfeld derides skinny people as "a nightmare of the high-fashion model of the late fifties and early sixties."

As you reel from K.L.'s outrageous inconsistencies, resist the temptation to become irate or dismissive. Take a moment to search for the deeper meanings therein.

In defense of the fan-jiggling couturier, it must be acknowledged that it is a glamorous eccentric's prerogative to change his or her mind. We should not look to creative types like Karl—coming as he does from the flighty, ephemeral world of fashion—for consistency.

Also in Karl's defense, it must be acknowledged that what passes for an ideal silhouette changes radically from epoch to epoch. One decade's zaftig ideal—think Shelley Winters in the '50s and '60s—is another decade's gasp-inducing blimp. Today's flat-chested megamodel could be tomorrow's Karen Carpenter tragedy.

However, if you put aside the vicissitudes of fashion for one moment, you will clearly see that there's a fabulously life-enhancing lesson in Kaiser Karl's about-face. What seems at first like treachery and hypocrisy is, in fact, nothing more than good old-fashioned healthy self-esteem.

Whether thin or fat, confident Mr. Lagerfeld has always remained his own most loyal proponent. His girth may fluctuate, but his belief in the essential correctness of Karl never does. When he's chubby, flesh is de rigueur; when he's thin, bones are in. Rather than be assailed for his fickleness, he's to be applauded for his *über alles* self-confidence. Take a tip from Karl—and from Shelley and Totie and all the big gals—and love the current you.

"I have things in my closet
that even I wouldn't wear!"

BETH RUDIN DeWOODY

*Art collector, philanthropist, mom, and New York
social fixture responds to the Eccentric Glamour
questionnaire.*

What are you wearing?

All white—I'm mad for white—with rock-and-roll bangles, an
insane orange rubber sculptural Gaetano Pesce ring, and a big
fat rock.

**When did you first realize that you might in fact be a
glamorous eccentric?**

Halloween! All the other posh little girls on the Upper East
Side came as ballerinas or princesses. I was always a hillbilly
with a chalked-up face and big beard or Li'l Abner. I remember
being embarrassed at first and then stopped caring.

Were your parents horrified?

My mother was amused. In the '60s when I was growing up
she was mod and slightly groovy. In 1966 she took me to get

a Vidal Sassoon haircut when he first came to America. It cost
$25, or maybe it was $50.

Are you prone to mood swings?
No, but I love mood rings.

**Have you ever been mocked for any of your glamorous
eccentricities?**
No, but they've been used as evidence in someone else's di-
vorce case.

What is the most eccentrically glam thing in your closet?
So many things! I have a vintage Pucci lime green empire dress
that was owned by Ginger Rogers. I love '60s futurist stuff:
There's an amazing Rudi Gernreich gold lamé jacket and one
of those incredible Paco Rabanne paillette dresses. I just bought
a handbag shaped like a hat, vintage Moschino. I have one of
his surreal runway outfits, with real knives and forks attached to
the jacket. I have things in my closet that even I wouldn't wear!
My eccentricity is also expressed in the art I collect and my collections of weird stuff: vintage Bettie Page photographs, and I
have a funny collection of butt plugs. They were advertised as
"medical devices to aid digestion." I'm sure they were sexual,
but I think they are sculptural.

**Have you ever wished you could trade in your life of
glamorous eccentricity for one of dreary conformity?**
At a certain point my kids started with that why-can't-you-be-
like-other-moms stuff. I told them, "When you're older, you
will be happy I am this way." Now my daughter steals everything out of my closet, including that Rudi Gernreich.

When does eccentric glamour become idiocy?
When people take it too seriously and forget to have fun.

Who is your inspirational icon of glamorous eccentricity?
Auntie Mame. The real key to her is how she reacted when she lost her shekels: She went and got a job, acting, selling roller skates, whatever! And she gave her last coin to Santa Claus. Her dignity and humor stayed intact in a bad situation. I would like to think I could do the same. And she never got stuck. She changed her ideas and her décor constantly. I can relate.

Do men think you are hot?
Absolutely!

What is the thing that most offends your glamorously eccentric sensibilities?
Intolerance, which brings us back to Auntie Mame. Remember how she fought against anti-Semitism and all that social climbing by her mundane in-laws?

Where do you wish to be buried, and in what?
I want to be cremated and placed in a Chinese rock crystal incense burner.

CHAPTER 13

Soothing or Annoying

The glam eccentric guide to love

Have you ever hung out in a small-town saloon or a dusty suburban mall or a Midwestern coffee shop? When you were there, did you happen to notice a hideous, unapologetically fat, blowsy woman with no teeth and a pierced navel?

Well, did you?

Yes, I knew it!

And this particular woman, though she may have been a perfectly lovely human being, did she look, to all intents and purposes, like Buddy Hackett in a tressy blond wig?

Well, did she?

And she had a scar, didn't she? And a child's face tattooed across her sunburned back, leading you to think that she might be, or have been at one point in her life, a biker chick.

And there was something else about this lady that stuck in your memory, wasn't there?

Come on, admit it.

You know what I'm talking about. Say it. Yes, she was with a man, wasn't she? And what was he like, this boyfriend, this companion? Come on, fess up! Was he toothless and scaly? Was he grotesque?

No, he wasn't, was he?

Admit it: He was the hottest-looking guy you have ever seen in your life. Am I right? Let me guess . . . face of George Clooney, body of Brad Pitt. *Bonjour!* I knew it.

And after you finally stopped staring at him, you looked at his lady friend, and then you looked at your infinitely more attractive self, reflected in a storefront or mirror, and you said to yourself (with a somewhat singsong Barbra-Streisand-in–*What's Up, Doc?* Jewish intonation), "*She* has a *boy*friend?"

We have all had the experience of spotting a rugged hunk with a hideous frowsy companion. Such couplings are frequently featured on the more confrontational daytime TV shows. It happens all the time. But have you ever stopped to think about what attracts these Patrick Dempseys to these behemoths? How does a woman who makes Quasimodo look like Sienna Miller manage to attract such a looker?

The answer is mystical and yet stunningly simple: What this gal and those of her genre have going for them is an unassailable belief in their own attractiveness.

Objectively, this lady may resemble Chris Farley—God rest his soul!—but she believes that she is a dead ringer for Naomi Watts.

She believes that, given enough liquor and the right lighting, Josh Hartnett or Jamie Foxx would abandon their significant others for her.

She believes that she is still in the running to become America's Next Top Model.

She believes with every fiber of her being and every tuft of her mustache that she is better looking and sexier than Pamela

Anderson and Marilyn Monroe combined and then multiplied by Jennifer Lopez.

And she believes it with such contagious ferocity that she creates a vacuum around her into which are sucked all the available men in a twenty-five-mile radius, including some really dishy ones.

Confidence, not physical perfection or power, is the ultimate aphrodisiac.

In our evil, elitist, looksist culture, there is a general feeling that such a woman is somehow not entitled to feel beautiful. Maybe this is a good moment to remind ourselves that beauty is subjective. Children and dogs and God do not discriminate against people based on their looks.

Wallflowers and Big Stinky Peonies

As you begin to dip your toes into the luscious lagoon of eccentric glamour, you will experience a jarring increase in the amount of amorous attention you receive. When you replace a limp wallflower with a giant, irresistible, gorgeously stinky peony, you will find that everyone wants to cop a sniff. The new laissez-faire stylish you, the self-invented rule breaker that you are becoming, will prove instantly more attractive to those you encounter than the previous you.

Is this a direct result of how fabulous and gorgeous you are? *Non!* It is simply a result of how gorgeous and fabulous you *think* you are.

So amp up that confidence and brace yourself for some serious fan worship. Once you start exuding all this newfound idiosyncrasy and self-love, men are going to whistle at you. Complete strangers are going to offer to pay for your Frappuccino. They are going to stare at your various areas and, if they are naughty, they are probably going to try to touch them. (If they don't, then you are probably in a gay neighborhood. More about that in a minute.)

Feeling overwhelmed at the prospect of this intrusive attention? Prefer to stay at home and watch *Dynasty* reruns? This is not an option. Having worked so hard to become a glamorous eccentric, you cannot be allowed to hide your new disco light under a bushel. It is all a waste of time—yours and mine—unless you share it with someone. It's a "Life's a banquet and most poor suckers are starving to death" Auntie Mame kind of a thing. Or, if you prefer a bit of Kande and Ebb, it's a "*What good is sitting alone in your room? Come hear the music play*" Liza in *Cabaret* kind of a thing.

Sizing Up the Competition

It's important to start out with a winner's mentality.

Whatever you do, don't allow yourself to be intimidated by any so-called competition, especially not by the Evas. I refer to that epidemic of ladies with the bleached hair and fake knockers described in Chapter 1.

These tacky broads have sacrificed any sense of individuality to turn themselves into man-trapping blow-up dolls. The Evas may appear at first glance to have a distinct advantage over a glam eccentric like you. Don't get discouraged by them. It is true that, because they look like whores, they have no problem getting men to fornicate enthusiastically with them. However, because these women all look alike, men cannot remember their names and constantly mix them up:

Hairy semiclad bloke scratching belly: "Good to see you, Yvette. Thanks for the laughs."

Tousled companion: "You son of a bitch! My name is Yvonne!"
(Slams motel door and stomps toward '77 Pontiac with drag-
ging muffler.)

Rest assured, this scenario will never happen to you.

Why?

Because you are an insanely more memorable individual.

Sorting the Chaps from the Chaff

Though I will not permit you to cringe away from your hordes
of new suitors, I cannot vouch for the quality thereof. There
could easily be some real duds in the bunch.

Some may want to show you a good time, some may only
want to show you dirty postcards.

Some may wear blousy pirate shirts from *International
Male* and try to woo you, à la Fabio, with lots of chest hair and
handmade chocolates. Others may feel it is enough to buy you
a Clark Bar. Somewhere in this smorgasbord, I guarantee that
you will find a quality product. The man of your dreams. It's
up to you to sort the chaps from the chaff.

Dudes and Poofs

When it comes to finding a life partner, the glamorous eccentric
has two choices open to her: She can marry either a "regular
guy" or a big screaming poof, a homosexual. It's just that simple.

Let's start with the regular guy, the good bloke, the normal
kind of dude.

A conventional man makes perfect sense for the glamorous eccentric. There is room for only one spotlight-grabber in
every household. And you're it. The last thing you want in a

man is some Weird Al Yankovic type who wants to borrow your eyeliner or upstage you at your annual block party.

There are higher concentrations of conventional men in some locations than in others. In order to speed up the whole process of finding your earnest, worthy mate, I would strongly advise you to propel yourself into as many obvious, straight, boring, male-dominated environments as possible.

If I were a woman—and I sincerely hope I never become one simply because it's so insanely more complicated than being a man—I would spend loads of time at Home Depot. Your visits to this national emporium will never be wasted. While you are cruising for Mr. Right, you can bone up on the latest advances in sheet rock construction. In need of a little exercise? The majestic Home Depot aisles are great for practicing your runway walk.

The highest concentration of "good men" is to be found in stadiums. One of my own man-trapping fantasy scenarios involves getting a part-time job selling Cokes and beer at sporting events.

In this scenario I see myself flirting with the spectators and sassing the competitors. What fun it would be to get into a spat with a highly strung cheerleader! The other servers would be jealous because, with my sense of fun and general savoir faire, I would get bigger tips and, eventually, a date with Mr. Right.

Mr. Right and I would then walk off into the sunset together, returning in glory to claim our front-row seats from which I would throw popcorn at my former co-workers.

Le Marriage Blanc

And now let's deal with the poofters. If lummoxy straight men are not your bag, don't panic. You still have another option: Marry a Mary.

This suggestion is aimed at women who are either past childbearing age or have low sex drive and no interest in procreation. If I were such a woman and I wasn't having any luck finding a good man, I would marry a good gay instead. Yes, a fabulous poofter. No question about it. The average gay, with his high tolerance for theatricality, maquillage, amd general silliness, is the perfect co-conspirator for a glamorous eccentric.

This kind of gay/straight union is not a new concept. The French call it a *marriage blanc*. I'm not sure why. I guess it is because, devoid of passion and red corpuscles, such a marriage is not really *rouge* and must therefore be *blanc*, the same bloodless color as the exquisite bone china that your new husband is bound to collect.

The fabulous upsides and advantages of *un marriage blanc* are almost too many to name. First, imagine how fab your house would be! It's no secret that the gays are full of nifty ideas for smartening up the home: It is, *après tout*, their screeching raison d'être. Even if money is tight, most homosexualists know their way round a staple gun and can, thanks to their innate verve, work miracles on even the most grim abode.

Regarding sex: As previously stated, if you are the kind of gal who is not really so into it, a gay is perfect for you. You slip into bed at night in matching jammies, safe in the knowledge that you are not about to be forced into one of those coiffure-destroying primitive positions while being obliged to yell absurd encouragements such as "Go, Daddy!" and "You're the king!" It's just not going to happen.

Life with a nellie is not all bedtime giggles and gourmet dinners; there are a couple of issues you must address before you throw in your lot.

Regarding hair: The average gay is overly fixated on hairdos. Your follicles can all too easily become his obsession. There is a strong possibility that he will begin to annoy you by constantly futzing with your coiffure. Hubby may try to rationalize his behavior by telling you he is trying to "create volume" or "reenergize your follicles." Either way, once he has started, it is always hard to get him to stop.

If your gay is getting hair-happy, I suggest that you immobilize him with a spritz of Aqua Net professional hairspray. On the average gay, this product has the same paralyzing effect as Mace.

Is he into show tunes?

If so, then exactly how much is he into show tunes? You do not want to spend the rest of your days listening to various cast recordings of *Pippin*.

Is he a crook?

Why is Julian/Jeremy/Sebastian marrying you? Most gays do not want to marry straight women. Does he have creepy ulterior motives? Maybe he's the heir to a vast fortune who will inherit money only if he makes a traditional union. Make sure you are in line for a slice of the action.

I make no apologies for my stereotyping of the gay population, or any other, for that matter, especially as the characteristics identified—creativity, a love of décor and good food—are all positives. Stereotypes are the lies that tell the truth.

Bend It with Beckham

If you cannot decide between a Home Depot hetero and a full-on hair-yanking homosexual, there are shades of gray available to you. I'm talking about that new breed of heterosissies. I'm talking about the original metrosexual, Mr. David Beckham.

Mr. Beckham is a great example of this genre. His poofy ways, including his penchant for traveling with scented candles, have been perennial fodder for the UK tabloids. An obsessive tidy queen, Beckham loves to rearrange the furniture in hotel rooms. His habit of offsetting pregame nerves with a calming manicure has earned him the nickname the Perfumed Ponce.*

Before you cast nasturtiums, bear in mind that his wife, the reed-thin Victoria Beckham, aka Posh Spice of the Spice Girls, attributes her slender figure to the fact that her candle-totin' husband is "an animal in bed." He's romantic, too: In a gesture reeking of old-fashioned working-class chivalry, Becks sends Posh a yellow rose every day. Awwh!

I Want to Marry Liberace

Another option: At some point during the long, drawn out gay marriage debate, a horrified dissenter suggested that our society was on the verge of a national moral collapse and that, if the gay marriage thingy was approved by Congress it would be only a matter of time before people wanted to—horror of horrors—marry their pets.

When I heard this, I gasped with incredulity. My partner, Jonathan Adler, and I have always wanted to enter into a polygamous union—minus any bestiality—with our Norwich terrier Liberace. We were just waiting for the powers that be to give us the go-ahead.

How could gay marriage critics not know that every single pet owner throughout history always wanted to marry his or her pet? Most consider their bond with their pet to be infinitely superior and more emotionally rewarding than anything they ever got from another *Homo sapiens.*

* Ponce: Old-fashioned Brit slang for pimp.

Pets are incredible. Pets are always ready with some positive feedback. Every glamorous eccentric needs a pet of some description to wag an approving tail when she throws on an outré outfit. Pets always think you look great. And they rarely try to hog the limelight. Pets will eat Spam while you eat steak. Pets are always ready with a lick. Pets think homeless people look great and smell great, that's how eccentrically glamorous pets are.

One final word . . .

Do not, whatever you do, worry about finding a smart man. Clever men are often prone to introspection The best men are—like happy Labrador dogs—a bit on the dopey side. Let beauty trump brains: Which brings us back to David Beckham, who apparently thought *pas de deux* meant "father of two." Bless him.

Despite his lack of intellect, Mr. Beckham has earned Posh's undying loyalty. When he publicly lamented, "Everyone thinks I'm stupid," Mrs. Beckham snapped back like a protective lioness, "Well, they're all ugly."

Talk to the hand . . . with the limp wrist.

Communicating Through the Hamster

Finding Mr. Right is a cause for celebration. A mild, low-key, tentative, nonelaborate sort of celebration. No floats. No fireworks. Keep the champagne in the cellar. Why the tepid lack of jubilation?

Finding a nice bloke is an accomplishment of sorts, but it's nothing compared with building, brick by brick, an eccentrically glamorous life together. Snagging your chap was a challenging diversion. Now that you've got him in your butterfly net, the real toil begins. Straight, gay, or in between, the chances are that he will not contribute much to the process. The burden of the creation of a stimulating shared life will fall to you. You must now take a blank, slightly turgid, work-focused individual and transform him into a world-class fun seeker.

He may take out the trash and unblock the gutters, but it's you—the rule-breaking, taboo-busting good-time gal that you have now become—who is going to add the sizzle and joie de vivre to your shared life. And it will require some effort. The same kind of ingenuity that you applied to the development of your personal style must now be channeled—times a million—into the creation of a beautiful "us."

The most important ingredient to a successful relationship is hostility. Let me rephrase that so it doesn't sound quite so vile. The most important ingredient of a successful relationship is the functional, creative expression of day-to-day hostilities. I'm not talking about a Jerry Springer scenario with flying fists, missing teeth, foul language, and torn brassieres. I'm not talking about Naomi-ing each other with cell phones and Black-Berrys. I'm not talking about Russell Crowe-ing each other with hotel front desk paraphernalia.

I'm talking about a certain nonviolent, functional state wherein a couple feels comfortable enough to highlight and to mock each other's foibles on a regular basis. This kind of mutual debunkery is the equivalent of deep breathing: It oxygenates a relationship and allows it to grow. The goal is to avoid those scenarios where unexpressed annoyances accumulate, turning you into Liz Taylor in *Who's Afraid of Virginia Woolf?* or, worse yet, Glenn Close in *Fatal Attraction*, or worserer yet Charlize Theron in *Monster*.

The best and most fun way to prevent grievances from accruing and becoming a nuclear threat is game playing. By inventing your own infantile and eccentric games—custom made to suit your particular relationship dynamic—you will build the foundation for a fabulous, loving future.

My husband and I have built quite an arsenal of these jolly japes. We have found that the best time to invent these kinds of insulting and mildly sadistic games is during our vacations. It gives one something to do. Who doesn't get a little bored while on vacation? What better way to fill up those long, empty hours than to think of creative ways to pillory one another?

Soothing or Annoying?

One year, while vacationing in Saint Barths, I invented a wonderful game that we dubbed *Soothing or Annoying?*

Though Soothing or Annoying? took about half an hour to invent, it has become an important load-bearing foundation in our relationship. Each year when our anniversary rolls around, I often pause and say to myself, "Aaah! All thanks to Soothing or Annoying?"

The rules of Soothing or Annoying? are quite simple. The most important thing to remember is that at no time should either party be allowed to feel soothed. Each player must dream up some heinously unsoothing physical torture which he or she can inflict on his opponent, using whatever tools are at hand: e.g., grinding the mesh of an adjacent tennis racket into the end of your loved one's nose, or whacking a calf with a wet rubber swimming flipper. The average bout should last no more than thirty seconds.

During the infliction of the Annoyance, the Annoyer must repeatedly ask the Annoyee, "Soothing or annoying?" The Annoyee wins or loses depending on his or her ability to endure the discomfort and maintain the lie that it feels "soothing." If the Annoyee capitulates before the thirty seconds are up, he or she automatically loses his or her turn to annoy.

Here are some more examples of acceptable annoyances: tapping your partner on the head with a long-stemmed dessert spoon; poking the temple with the sharp corner of a manila envelope or restaurant menu; stuffing handy greenery, such as house plants or fresh arugula, up the Annoyee's nostrils.

Try not to ratchet up the hostility too much. Anything that leaves unsightly welts or draws blood is verboten.

When you tire of Soothing or Annoying?—after four or five bouts, most couples are ready to call it quits—you can try a few rounds of another of my favorite games.

Concerto

It's quite a simple game and not dissimilar from Soothing or Annoying? in that it involves the infliction of as much annoyance as possible on someone you purport to love, this time under the guise of "making art."

A sound track is necessary for this game. A CD of a favorite classical piece, preferably one with a complex orchestration, is ideal. If there are outdoor concerts in your area, this is even better: You will have a guaranteed audience for your game.

Start the music. The two players face one another and flip a coin. The winner approaches the loser and begins to "play" his or her body in time to the music, as if it were a musical instrument.

Imagine that every aspect of your partner's body represents a different part of the orchestra. Nothing is off limits. Noses can be twanged like double bass strings, love handles can be fingered ferociously as if they were piano keys, the top of a head can become a bongo drum.

When the *Instrument* starts to whine and complain about

the irritating nature of the game, the *Musician* must counter these protests by vociferously defending his or her right to make art:

"Shh! I'm creating! How dare you! This is my art! Why would you want to prevent me from having freedom of expression? What kind of person are you?"

Though undeniably hilarious, this game is extremely hard to judge. There are no real winners or losers. The only way to make it fair is to alternate the bouts.

Re the score: If you hate classical music, feel free to use gangsta rap or '70s funk instead. The insistent beats will give you ample opportunity for much vigorous tickling and thwapping.

Innocent bystanders are often appalled by both Soothing or Annoying? and Concerto. Ignore them. It does not matter what they think: The important thing is that you, the two players, experience spiritual growth and closeness.

Who Knew Chihuahuas Could Have Such a Mouth on Them?

The most efficacious game which we invented—the ne plus ultra of therapeutic activity—is called *Talking Through the Hamster* and, *quelle surprise*, it requires owning a pet.

Though it's called Talking Through the Hamster, this game rarely involves one of those honey-colored little charmers. Most people will, due to their ubiquity, use a dog or a cat. I dubbed it Talking Through the Hamster—TTTH for short—in order to emphasize that there was no limit to the scale or intellectual level of the animal in question. You can play this game whether your pet is a buffalo or a stick insect. TTTH is nothing if not inclusive.

Start by giving your pet a voice.

This can come out of nowhere or be based on some aspect of the pet personality or provenance. My dog Liberace is a tough little Norwich terrier: I gave him, therefore, the voice of an English working-class yobbo. Since Liberace was castrated at a fairly young age, I dragged the voice up a couple of octaves to a match that of a slightly irate UK housewife.

Phase one. Most people ask their pet questions: "Are you a hungry gal?" "Who's the most beautiful boy?" but not everyone has what it takes to channel his or her pet's voice and actually to answer those questions. By doing this you are becoming a ventriloquist of sorts. Instead of a Charlie McCarthy doll you have a real flesh-and-blood animal to play with.

You are well on your way to being able to play TTTH.

After a week of ventriloquizing via your pet, you are now ready to graduate from merely answering on behalf of your pet to making bold statements. These could relate to the weather or to geopolitical matters. Liberace can now comment on everything from Oscar fashions—"She's mutton dressed as lamb!"—to international geopolitical turmoil—"Why doesn't the Taliban like dogs?"

Gradually and organically, an independent personality will emerge.

Phase two. Once your pet's voice is established, the important work can begin. You can now use your pet to say critical things about your boyfriend or husband which, if they came directly from your mouth, would be a little too abrasive—not to mention accurate—for comfort.

Here are some examples of things your pet might say. For your convenience I have paired these verbal assaults with the circumstances under which such statements might be appropriate.

Example: Your husband's love of food is causing him to

pack on the pounds. He's a nibbler. Every time he enters or leaves the house, he makes a pit stop at the refrigerator for a little *quelque chose.*

On seeing your loved one stuffing his third ice-cream sandwich into his mouth, Your pet says (via you): "Paging Richard Simmons!"

Before your husband can become hurt or irate, or remind you that you yourself are no stranger to the refrigerator, you leap to his defense and castigate the impudent beast: "Boy, who knew Chihuahuas could have such a mouth on them." In the meantime, I guarantee you that the ice-cream sandwich will be back in the freezer before you can say "gastric bypass."

Example: Your husband, though delightful in many ways, is crucifyingly long-winded. Most men tend to be a trifle bombastic. Whenever you have company, he launches into a horrifyingly drawn-out anecdote. You love him, so you are reluctant to attempt to curb this behavior with a deflationary criticism in front of guests. Your pet, however, has no such genteel qualms. When your husband is going full throttle on that tired old story about how you got the price of the house down from $122,000 to $121,000, your pet says (via you), "Shorter! Funnier!" or, "Anyone got a cyanide capsule handy?"

Before your husband has time to be hurt, you once more leap in to take his part, cautioning your pet that any further outbursts will result in a withholding of tomorrow's treats.

Spoken in the accented croak of your iguana, or the treacly purr of your Siamese cat, these sarcastic assaults are the stealth missiles that enable you to shape your bloke's behavior in a nonthreatening eccentrically glamorous way.

After a year or so of hearing you ventriloquizing via your pet, do not be surprised if your husband learns to imitate Rover or Polly's voice and starts to throw it right back at you. Your attempts at nouvelle cuisine, your penchant for unflattering pegged pants, your annoyingly flamboyant arm gestures will all become grist to his mill.

If this becomes unbearable, you can claim that Fluffy the shih tzu has been subjected to a great shock—an attempted rape by that nasty Weimaraner from number 15—and that Fluffy is now mute. It will be a few days before your guileless husband figures out that, while you were away visiting your mother, a lightning storm descended on the city, the shock of which miraculously restored Fluffy's voice. But when he does, watch out!

By the time you two reach your glamorously eccentric old age, you will be seasoned players. I can see you both now, appalling the other inmates at your old folks' home with your endless rounds of Concerto. Every morning you castigate your little shih tzu for commenting on your loved one's loose dentures. He looks back at you with love and adoration . . . and then grabs your knitting needles for a quick bout of Soothing or Annoying?

Ah! True love!

*"I mock myself for the **Matrix** trench coat, Doc Martens, black eyeliner, 'Riunite on ice' look I had in high school."*

LUCY LIU

The Anna May Wong of the twenty-first century, the most glamorous Asian eccentric ever to emerge from the streets of Queens responds to the Eccentric Glamour questionnaire.

What are you wearing?
Black Evisu AG celebration jeans and a Rachel Roy Elizabethan collared cotton shirt with Christian Louboutin silver, gold, and black patent deco-inspired sling-backs.

When did you first realize that you might in fact be a glamorous eccentric?
When Canal Street Jeans was my mecca and I wore only one-of-a-kind thrift store pieces that were no doubt original but also had that oh-so-chic *parfum de* mothball.

Were your parents horrified?
They built a shrine and had a ritual bonfire every Shabbat and burned shoulder-padded Ralph Lauren pussy-cat-bowed suits

as an offering to my ancestors in hopes that they'd impress upon me via dreams, visions, etc., to dress as a dutiful Chinese daughter who was not a punk rocker. Saving face is everything in Chinese culture.

Are you prone to mood swings?
No. Yes. Maybe. Why're you asking me so many questions?!

Have you ever been mocked for any of your glamorous eccentricities?
I mock myself for the *Matrix* trench coat, Doc Martens, black eyeliner, "Riunite on ice" look I had in high school. Let's not forget the Duran Duran "her name is Rio" hair-sprayed bangs that completed the ensemble.

What is the most eccentrically glam thing in your closet?
A nineteenth-century exquisitely fitted camel-colored wool riding jacket with tortoiseshell buttons and elaborate appliqué detailing.

Have you ever wished you could trade in your life of glamorous eccentricity for one of dreary conformity?
Never.

When does eccentric glamour become idiocy?
Are thirty-two pairs of black Louboutin shoes idiocy? I don't know.

Who is your inspirational icon of glamorous eccentricity?
Babe Paley, Audrey Hepburn, Shakira Caine, Anna Piaggi, Isabella Blow.

Do men think you are hot?
Duh.

What is the thing that most offends your glamorously eccentric sensibilities?
When people limit their imagination to thinking only the most expensive things in the world are chic. I love to mix and match—it's important not to forget the 718 even when you live in the 212 or the 310.

Where do you wish to be buried, and in what?
I wish be to be cryogenically frozen in Nan Kempner's closet, and when I wake up, I can choose from her incredible collection.

CHAPTER 14

Splash Your Breasts
with Ice-Cold Water

Lousy advice with chilling consequences

There's nothing quite like the first time. You might forget the second or the third. But not the first time. Everyone remembers it. I know I will never forget my first time. I am talking, of course, about the first time I was ever given a piece of really crappy advice.

My sister Shelagh and I are standing in the backyard of our childhood home.

"Close your lips really tight. Do it!"

I have no idea why Shelagh wants me to lock lips with our filthy, prewar green rubber garden hose. Shouldn't she be watering the herbaceous borders, as per my mother's instructions?

"Now, close your eyes."

I obey my sister. She, like so many of the great dictators of history, deploys a warm and encouraging tone. This deceptive delivery hypnotizes the victim and leads him or her to believe that the persecutor has only the victim's best interests at heart, and that any questioning will only delay what must certainly be a positive outcome.

"Keep quiet. Now, without opening your mouth, I want you to slowly count to five."

"One. Two. . . ."

I hear the squeak of the rusty garden faucet being turned, followed, milliseconds later, by a massive oral deluge.

"Threeeeeeeeeeeaaaahhyyaow!"

Suddenly I feel as if my skull is exploding. Forty gallons of H_2O have entered my body. I cough and splutter, and I open my eyes. My sister is rocking with laughter. My nasal passages, lungs, ears, stomach have been machine-gunned with high-velocity freezing-cold water.

"Okay. Let's do it again. Only this time let's see if you can keep the hose inside your mouth for longer."

"Why?"

"Okay. Stick it in. Good. Now start counting . . ."

Looking back fondly, I realize that every exciting eventuality in my life, regardless of how much discomfort was involved, has been precipitated by a reckless or malevolent piece of advice. The bad dates, the skin rashes, the freak accidents, the blush-making style excesses—all the really character-building stuff!—seem to have occurred after heeding a really crappy suggestion from some "well-meaning" friend or relative.

And I survived them all, stronger and fitter, with my life invariably enhanced in some way or other.

Bad advice is, therefore, something of a misnomer.

Like bad taste, a dollop of bad advice is really quite necessary, especially for the glamorous eccentric. It's important to give it. It's important to receive it. In many ways, bad advice

238

is, especially for an unconventional gal, good advice in disguise. I find it odd that Darwin's theories contain no mention of the critical role played by lousy advice. After all, the only way to test those theories of natural selection is to catapult somebody into a sink-or-swim challenging situation. And what better way to observe the survival of the fittest than by monitoring the fallout from a piece of dreadful advice?

To those who would disagree, I say this: Imagine a world without bad advice. Imagine, if you will, a utopia where people mind their own business. Imagine a world where a friend will not advise another friend to "get an asymmetrical haircut" or "splash your breasts with ice-cold water" or "try one of those molasses and wheat germ colonics." Imagine a world where nobody tells anybody to shave a shamrock into a private area or learn to play the zither.

What would it be like?

Close your eyes and allow a vision of this edict-free, dreamy land to take shape in your mind's eye.

At first it seems like paradise: no broken hearts or cracked shins. No white knuckles or red-faced humiliations.

Squint and try to envisage the look and feel of this brave new world, a world where people function happily without the promptings of others.

It's a misty sort of place. There's not a lot going on. In fact, if you look carefully you'll see that the landscape looks a trifle bleak. Stagnant, even. Nothing is happening and nobody is moving or talking. The mise-en-scène recalls the scene in the sci-fi cult classic *Logan's Run* featuring the Apathetics, lazy hippie-looking slobs who just lie around all day looking as if they have been shot with *Daktari* tranquilizer darts. It's a vacuum. A black hole.

The truth is, without a constant flow of wacky suggestions flying back forth, all meaningful activity, from liver transplants to cake decorating, would come screeching to a halt. Without a barrage of goading advice, we Earthlings would just sit around eating lotuses and watching telly, except there would not be any telly because nobody would have advised anyone to invent it. We would fester and rot and watch the clock while bluebottle flies crawled across our unimaginatively attired, indolent bodies. Advice, bad advice in particular, is vital for our survival.

The baddest thing about bad advice is that you never see it coming. Bad advice is always mislabeled. It doesn't come in a package labeled "bad advice." It's like eating spinach leaves and contracting *E. coli*. You would never eat the spinach if it were packaged as "Delicious spinach with extra *E. coli*."

Bad advice always comes packaged as good advice. You never know it's bad until you are wincing in pain or writhing with embarrassment. This adds to the surprise and excitement of really, really bad advice.

There's Nothing Like a Good Cringe

Once upon a time I found myself at a Barneys store opening party with a group of friends. Across the room, ogled by us, sat Sharon Stone. She was perched on a black cocktail stool, nursing a half-drunk flute of champagne in a confident, knowing sort of way.

"I am the most fabulously bitchy and glamorous actress in the history of the cinema. You know it and I know it, and that's why you love me," her expression seemed to say.

La Stone was wearing a glitzy black tube top and pants; there was, therefore, no chance of her flashing her *Basic Instinct*. Not that I cared. I was far more interested in inspecting her psyche than her nether regions. I was desperate to know if she was as ruthless and intimidating as Catherine Tramell. How much of Ginger, the dope-crazed bombshell from *Casino*, was lurking in the real Sharon? Was she as cold and calculating as Miss Horner, the evil schoolteacher in the mauve sweater set from *Diabolique*?

She runs her hand through her choppy urchin hairdo, tosses back her head and, on hearing some witticism from her companion, lets forth one of those Sharon Stonian peals of laughter that are such a big part of that public awards show personality, the one she uses to hide all the evil ones that I know in my heart of hearts constitute the real her.

"Why don't you go and talk to her?" asks an adjacent colleague.

"Me?" I reply, theatrically splaying a nervous hand across my upper chest.

"You're so obsessed with her. Don't you want to find out what she's like?" demands another.

"It's simple. Tell her you work for Barneys and you just want to hang out with her!" shrieks another, as Sharon-mania ignites our entire table.

"Yes, go tell her we *all* want to hang with her."

"Invite her over! She can only say no."

"There's a spare chair right here. Do it!"

"Do it!"

"Do it! Do it! Do it! Do it!"

This avalanche of good advice works its pernicious magic on my squishy brain. The "do its" are stated with such coercive enthusiasm that the whole notion of befriending Miss Stone begins to seem not just feasible but necessary and important. Propelled by this ghastly counsel, I am now at some halfway point between my old life, sans Sharon, and a fabulous, new Sharon-centered existence. There's no turning back.

Unconsciously, I find myself lurching to my feet and stumbling toward the gamine glamour-puss like a drunk staggering into traffic. I reach her shins and look up. Perched high on her cocktail stool, she is about four feet taller than me. I am completely out of her field of vision. She is totally unaware of my presence.

"Hello there!" I holler up, in a spirited, hearty way.

Grudgingly, Miss Stone lowers her gaze and angles it in my direction.

"My friends and I love you and . . ."

Sharon Stone raises an eyebrow, which is no doubt plucked by that bloke who has become famous for doing all the Hollywood brows.

"We thought it would be awfully good fun if you . . ."

I hear myself sounding more and more like a flustered English spinster inviting the handsome new vicar over for some tea and cucumber sandwiches for the first time.

". . . when you come off stage . . . it would just be so marvelous . . . if you would come and sit with us so that we might . . . get to know you?"

Nothing.

". . . so, if you have a minute, it would be just great . . . and . . ."

Without the slightest glimmer of emotion, Miss Stone puts me out of my misery.

"No thanks," she says.

She recrosses her legs and raises her gaze.

There's a painful silence.

I can feel the expectant eyes of all my goading colleagues burning into my back like the fangs of a billion poisonous asps.

Slowly but surely, every orifice of my body begins to contract with hideous cringing embarrassment. If cringing made a noise like, for example, shattering glass, Sharon and I and the entire room would all have our hands over our ears, such is the magnitude of my cringe fest. But it doesn't. Cringing is silent, painfully silent.

"Okay. Well, thanks anyway," I say while simultaneously praying that I have not become incontinent. "You have a nice evening."

I pause slightly, waiting for a "you too." There is nothing. Just the confident stare of a woman who does not care if I live or die.

Death, I ponder as I waddle ignominiously back to my table, is infinitely preferable to the overwhelming, bowel-curdling embarrassment that I am currently feeling.

Vengeful feelings begin to meld with my feelings of shame. I resolve not to meet my maker alone. I will take others with me.

Upon reaching my seat, I am barraged with questions. I ignore them. I smile at my team of helpful advisers and silently vow to destroy them. They, with their horrifyingly stupid suggestions, are, I now realize, the cause of my misery and all the misery that exists in the world. I will murder them all with an ice pick, à la Sharon. Then I will throw myself in front of Sharon's Alfa Romeo, and we will all die because we deserve to die, because Sharon Stone thinks we suck.

The aftermath of lousy advice can be complex. Sometimes there are hospital bills to be paid. Sometimes there are legal matters to be resolved. But more often than not the damage is emotional rather than physical or financial. Time is a great healer. As the mists clear and the agonies subside, you come to realize that what you actually received was not bad advice, but good advice in disguise.

Eventually the Sharon wounds healed. After a few days I began to "put back the pieces" and move on with my life. Ere long I was able to extract something positive from my Sharon experience.

I took satisfaction from the fact that La Stone had, during our brief interview, revealed herself to be every bit as fabulously haughty and grand as I had ever wanted her to be. If she had let down her guard and spent the evening "shooting the shit" with a bunch of us fawning acolytes, she would undoubtedly have deconstructed herself and lost her mystique. My image of her was intact.

It's a Totally Heavy Scene, Man

The advice game works both ways. For the glamorous eccentric, doling it out is just as important as receiving it, if not more so. This is because you are more imaginative than other people. Your ability to concoct wild schemes and think outside *la boîte* makes you uniquely qualified to produce an endless stream of wacky suggestions that will shake up the lives of the less fortunate.

Your mission is to propel your fellow human beings off their couches—thereby preventing bedsores—and force them into memorable and challenging situations. Don't hold back. You will enjoy it. Trust me: Giving ill-considered advice is definitely more fun than giving earnest, wholesome, tried-and-true advice. I know whereof I speak. Don't let the garden hose and Sharon Stone anecdote fool you. I have doled out more than my fair share of horrible suggestions, with invariably gruesome consequences.

What about the time, back in the glam-rock 1970s, I insisted my transvestite roommate run across the street to catch a bus when he was wearing a full-length gown—and he wasn't wearing his glasses—and he fell over a low, swagged chain fence?

His mangled shins swelled to the size of beer barrels. He couldn't even squeeze them into his cerise chiffon palazzo pants.

This testing encounter with fate taught him so much: He learned about his own pain threshold; he learned about the intrinsic dangers of chiffon. In retrospect I almost feel as if I should have invoiced him.

Then there was my first time. Ah! You can never forget that first time.

The very first piece of dreadful advice I ever doled out was directed at a couple of teen runaways. It was a really heavy scene. (The word "heavy" was, at this point in the late 1960s, thrown around like one of Janis Joplin's marabou boas.) He was my best friend at school and she was a local factory girl who was "in a friendless condition," courtesy of my friend. This in itself was heavy enough. Thanks to me, it was about to get much heavier.

Their names were Rita and Tony. Scared of parental wrath, the two star-crossed lovers were totally at a loss. What should they do? Where should they go?

Foolishly, they turned to me. They actually asked me for advice.

I found this extremely heavy. It was the Summer of Love, or thereabouts. I was sixteen. Nobody had ever asked me for any advice before. I was also flattered. It gave me a weird sense of heavy omnipotence.

Instantly I came up with a brilliant suggestion: I told Rita and Tony to head immediately to Glastonbury, the site of Britain's big annual music festival. By the time the solstice rolled around, the whole place would be filled with druids and caring flower children who would share their food and other resources. It would be totally heavy, but in a positive way.

At my suggestion, they packed a beige vinyl suitcase—stolen from Rita's mum—and split the scene, man. The suitcase was totally heavy, literally and figuratively. They had filled it with canned goods stolen from their family larders.

They did not get far. Rita and Tony were nabbed by the police while wandering aimlessly around Glastonbury and looking for druids. They were ID'd by the heavy beige vinyl suitcase.

Our reunion, a couple of days later, was not quite the love fest that I had anticipated. It was, in fact, quite heavy.

"You wanker!" yelled Tony in a menacing and unhippielike way. "The solstice happens in the summer. It's the summer solstice!"

"It's nine months away," added Rita, touching her expanding

and heavy belly. "How were we supposed to survive the bloody winter?"

Though my advice was flawed and impractical, it had ultimately turned out to be good advice. I had, albeit very indirectly, facilitated a kumbaya with the hapless lovers and their respective families. The facts of the situation were now on the table.

And, most important, my rotten suggestions had sent my two chums off on an unforgettable adventure. My advice had a sense of romance. It had verve. It had panache!

Picnicking with Rabid Raccoons

Much of the advice that is doled out to women today is decidedly panache free. It's mundane. It's cautious. It's riddled with PC disclaimers and warnings. Worst of all, it lacks imagination and a sense of infinite possibilities. "Start online banking today!" "Minimize your UV exposure!" Yawn!

If you are going to go to the trouble of inflicting advice on somebody else, at least have the decency to be imaginative.

Want to catapult a depressed friend into an inspirational situation?

"What you need is a clothing-optional vacation!"

In the mood to subject a colleague to some fashion experimentation?

"Cut the sleeves off that trench coat and wear it as a dress!"

See a pal who's in need of a lifestyle change?

"Adopt an abandoned psychotic marmoset!"

As a glamorous eccentric, it is your obligation to give advice that is exciting and challenging.

How about doling out some relationship advice for Valentine's Day?

"What the hell! Marry that one-legged asylum-seeker neighbor of yours! There's nobody else on the horizon. Why not?"

Don't sit on the sidelines! Join in the fun! The key is to give as good as you get! Catapult a friend into a challenging situation! Send someone off to chat to Sharon Stone! Better yet, try Courtney Love. I hear she loves to meet her fans first thing in the morning. Drop by with some Dunkin' Donuts and bang, really, really loudly, on her front door. Give it a whirl!

I would love to see us all return to the halcyon days when Diana Vreeland—that patron saint of glamorous eccentrics and of fabulously inspiring advice—famously screeched reckless edicts from her "Why don't you . . . ?" column in *Harper's Bazaar.*

"Why don't you . . . waft a big bouquet around like a fairy wand?"

"Why don't you . . . have a white monkey-fur bed cover mounted on yellow velvet?"

"Why don't you . . . have your cigarettes stamped with a personal insignia?"

"Why don't you . . . wear violet velvet mittens with everything?"

Her advice was crazy and bankrupting yet totally life enhancing and life affirming. If you followed it, you always ran the risk of being carted away by men in white coats or arrested ("Your honor, the defendant, who was wearing violet velvet mittens at the time, was observed brandishing a floral bouquet in a menacing fashion . . .") But so what? At least Mrs. Vreeland's advice was never *ordinaire.* When she told you to "drag your Aubusson rug to a waterfall and have a picnic," she did not care if you got eaten by rabid raccoons or killed by falling rocks or shot at by Unabomber-type people with banjos. She knew that your alfresco lunch would be so utterly fabulous that any bloodshed or mayhem was totally justified.

"I failed to notice that the trailing end of a blue chiffon scarf I had knotted insouciantly at my neck had caught in the turntable, and the next thing I knew my face was smack against the spinning disc and I was gasping for air."

HAMISH BOWLES

Vogue editor-at-large, couture collector, wit,
and bon viveur responds to the Eccentric Glamour
questionnaire.

What are you wearing?

Chartreuse seersucker suit, lavender shirt, "monkey king" cuff links that Tony Duquette made for Tyrone Power, rose-sprigged lavender tie, silver and bottle-green serpent belt from the German hippies in Santa Gertrudis in Ibiza, lavender socks from the Tangier souk, and ancient Lobb shoes.

When did you first realize that you might in fact be a glamorous eccentric?

When I nearly died an Isadora Duncan death aged nine, while listening to a Gertrude Lawrence 78 on a windup gramophone I had compelled my parents to buy me. Lost in the evocative magic of La Lawrence's crackling trills, I failed to notice that the trailing end of a blue chiffon scarf I had knotted insouciantly at my neck had caught in the turntable, and the next thing I knew my face was smack against the spinning disc and I was gasping for air. Happily, I just had a moment in hand to lunge for the "off" dial. Glamorously eccentric death rather narrowly avoided.

Were your parents horrified?

My parents were highly supportive. If they were alarmed at my channeling Gladys Cooper in *My Fair Lady* as a preteen, they sweetly never let on.

Are you prone to mood swings?

Not really. But I do get terribly excited if I find an unlabeled Cristobal Balenciaga at the thrift store.

Have you ever been mocked for any of your glamorous eccentricities?

I wore a burgundy pin-striped skirt (fetchingly cut to the knee, gaiters) that John Galliano made for me to the Paris collections in about 1984. In retrospect I think the French cabdrivers were hostile, but at the time I don't believe I thought for one minute the catcalls and hollering could possibly have been directed at *moi*.

What is the most eccentrically glam thing in your closet?

A Philip Treacy violet whirling dervish fez sprouting a panache of flame-colored bird-of-paradise plumes and a detachable yashmak made from tarnished silver coins.

Have you ever wished you could trade in your life of glamorous eccentricity for one of dreary conformity?

No.

ECCENTRIC GLAMOUR

When does eccentric glamour become idiocy?
When it is studied or self-conscious.

Who is your inspirational icon of glamorous eccentricity?
Isabella Blow was and always will be, although she loathed the
word "eccentric."

Do women think you are hot?
Oddly enough, they sometimes do. It is very disquieting.

**What is the thing that most offends your glamorously
eccentric sensibilities?**
The way people dress for the theater and international air
travel.

Where do you wish to be buried, and in what?
At Saint Andrews' Church in Tangier in a lavender djellaba.

CHAPTER 15

Dressing Down Is a Crime Against Humanity

Don't hide your eccentric glamour under a bushel

You have now, if you have been paying attention, joined the ranks of the eccentrically glamorous. Be proud. It's an achievement. You have reimagined, reinvented, and revitalized your personal style and—wow!—you managed to do it without turning into a hoochie blow-up doll. Mazel tov!

Whether in the Existentialist, Socialite, or Gypsy category, you are now armed with a very clear sense of your own very clear idiosyncratic self. You have *le chien*. Woof! Feels good, doesn't it.

Was it as difficult as you thought? Probably not. Trading in your old life for one of eccentric glamour has, after all, an intrinsic logic to it. Why would you want to look nondescript when you could look fierce?

Why would you want to wear an institutional-looking itchy

flannel A-line prison wardress suit when there's a set of unworn, lightly beaded, mint-green crêpe de chine hostess pajamas in a drawer in your closet?

Why wear a heavy, heathered, sludge-colored shetland mock-turtle when there's a feather-light, tangerine angora cardigan with rhinestone buttons at your disposal?

Why wear bunion-friendly sneakers when gold strappy evening sandals are, after a couple of martinis, just as comfortable? Why wear one strand of pearls when eleven make more noise?

Why wear a greige career suit when a black leotard, forest-green crocodile thigh boots, and a Peruvian mini-poncho are beckoning to you?

It's not hard to resist tuna melts once you have nibbled a few crêpes suzette.

But don't get too smug too soon.

There will be moments when you—yes, the new insanely more fabulous you—will freak out and abandon the courageous path you have chosen. You will lose your nerve. You will falter. You will desert your post.

To ram home my point, I will tell a monumentally cautionary tale. This story clearly demonstrates that nobody is safe: Even the most eccentrically glamorous among us can occasionally backslide. A lady can, if the circumstances are dire enough, lose sight of the complete and utter pointlessness of caring about what others think and capitulate to the pressure to conform.

This is not okay. These kinds of relapses are totally unacceptable. When she falls off the wagon, the glamorous eccentric lets down not just herself but the entire universe. Naughty, inconsistent glamorous eccentric!

Belfast, 1962

Jackie Kennedy is in the White House, and I'm not. We Doonans are across the Atlantic enjoying our annual vacation in sunnyish Northern Ireland with my monosyllabic, hard-drinking grandfather. I am ten years old.

One morning my mother Betty informs us that today we will break the rainy monotony with a day trip. Our destination is a far homestead inhabited by some of our relatives. Betty describes them as "good people," which bodes well. Anything that Betty describes as "good" invariably has a whiff of glamour to it.

The preparations are intense. We all take baths. This necessitates taking the junk out of the tub and boiling endless kettles of water. Normally, while sojourning with my granddad, we did not bathe much. Why would we? Our personal hygiene is maintained by daily frolics in the oily polluted waters of Belfast Lough.

While Betty irons our shirts and combs our hair, my dad brushes his suede Hush Puppies. All the adults scrub and insert their dentures. I am happy. I like the idea that we are all getting "tarted up."

To *tart up,* to be a *tart,* to *tart* something *up,* to *tart* yourself *up*—these phrases are frequently heard during my childhood. Though clearly deriving from "tart," as in a prostitute, as in streetwalker, the verb "to tart" has only positive connotations. To tart things up is to banish postwar grimness with a dash of Technicolor modernity. When something becomes tarted up—a person, a street, a front yard, a living room—it gets a new lease on life. Dusty austerity is replaced with shiny optimism. The humdrum is vanquished by the snazzy. Neglect is replaced with mascara.

The adjective "tarty" has less favorable connotations. If thus described, one can safely assume that a particular lady has, when engaged in the otherwise harmless pursuit of tarting herself up, gone too far. Or maybe she is a bona fide tart, in which case she has simply costumed herself for work.

Lest I confuse, permit me to emphasize the difference between dressing slutty and tarting yourself up. While dressing slutty—the horrifyingly ubiquitous contemporary version of which was the springboard for this book—denotes a full-on commitment to porno-chic and hoochie style, tarting oneself up connotes a life-enhancing commitment to flair, adornment, and eccentric glamour. Whether you are an Existentialist, a Socialite, or a Gypsy, you are entitled to your fair share of sizzle and panache. You are entitled to tart yourself up. Just don't go too far, that's all.

Back to Betty.

After she has given us all the once-over, my mother grabs a cup of tea, lights a fag, and retreats to her bedroom "to tart meself up a bit." Mrs. Doonan—the pièce de résistance of any outing—has saved herself for last.

Half an hour goes by. An hour.

I do not mind waiting. On the contrary; I like the idea that my mother, the glam eccentric with the improbable vintage '40s style, is going to knock 'em dead with a whole heapin' helpin' of her particular brand of style and pizzazz.

The sun comes out. Bees buzz. It's going to be a fine day. Maybe my mother will wear one of her bustier sun tops with a pencil skirt and white spike heels.

We stand in the front yard waiting for her big entrance, doing nothing much. Our hands are at our sides or in our pockets. It is the 1960s. People often stood about doing nothing while staring into the middle distance. There are no cell phones to whip out or iPods to twiddle. It is enough to be out of doors. Being out of doors, just like being indoors, is a legitimate activity. There is no pressure to be more meaningfully occupied. To this day I have retained this ability to do nothing and consider it an important part of my personal beauty regimen. Now, when people say, "You look great for your age. What's your secret?" I always reply, "Green tea and staring into the middle distance as often as possible."

Caution: Doing nothing is so totally out of whack with the crazed techie culture of our time that people will invariably misconstrue your motives. Bystanders will assume you are either on day release from a loony bin or ill-intentioned in some unimaginably horrid way. Once, when I was in the middle of doing nothing, someone asked me if I was having a stroke.

"Wur the haal is Batty?" growls Betty's dad in his incomprehensibly thick North Irish accent.

Suddenly he stops doing nothing and bangs on Betty's bedroom window with his huge gnarled peasanty hand. (It was a bungalow.)

"Wahl yeh gammy a mannut!" responds Betty loudly and irritably.

More doing nothing.

Ten minutes later the front door opens.

Out steps somebody quite unfamiliar.

Gone is the nail varnish.

Gone is the meringue of blond hair.

Gone is the boldly applied lipstick and mascara.

Gone are the chunky gold and fake-pearl earrings, the jangly charm bracelet.

Gone are the seamed stockings.

Gone are the white spike heels and matching purse.

Gone is the tartiness.

Gone is Betty.

The depressing apparition before us is a pale shadow of Betty's former self. To say Betty looked dowdy would be a horrifying understatement.

She is wearing one of my dead grandmother's old midcalf gray skirts. On her feet are flat shoes, borrowed from Auntie Muriel, a Belfast policewoman. Thick surgical hose cover her shapely legs. On the top is a navy and white cardigan that Betty normally wears as part of a crisp snappy nautical ensemble. Teamed with the gray skirt it now looked positively institutional.

"Your fingers look funny," says my sister Shelagh. Neither of us has ever seen my mother's nails before: They are always hidden by a thick coat of vermilion varnish. Having hastily wiped off the color only seconds before, Betty now reeks of acetone, as opposed to Nina Ricci's *L'Air du Temps*, her signature fragrance.

"*They* don't like nail polish. *They* think it's tarty," says my mother in a tone of barely concealed resentment. In tandem with her appearance, her mood has gone from fabulous to dour.

"Where is your hair?" I ask. Betty's proud 1940s pompadour is squished under a tightly knotted headscarf.

"*They* think blonde is tarty."

I begin to have misgivings about this trip. After ten years of observing Betty, I have a high comfort level with anything and everything that has been tarted up. This aversion to any kind of up-tarting is very alien to me. I had hoped, by embracing these new relatives, to increase the glamour quotient in our family, not decrease it.

The bumpy bus ride takes us from Belfast to Antrim. From

here we take a taxi to the back of beyond. It stops at the bottom of a long lane. In the distance is a humble cluster of white farmers' cottages. As we trudge up the hill, Betty, smoking what is to be her last cigarette for about six hours, gives us a little backstory on these good people, our people.

Most noteworthy among her tidbits is the fact that they function without gas or electricity or indoor plumbing. They live off the land and throw lumps of dried peat on the fire in order to keep warm. To my already fashion-obsessed ears, all this sounds quite grim and shockingly untarty.

As we approach the main cottage of the good people, various women come forward to greet us. They too wear knee-length gray skirts. These ladies are soft-spoken and so monumentally untarty that they make Betty, even de-tarted Betty, look ever so slightly tarty, proving, if nothing else, that tartiness will out.

It was a surreal kind of a day.

First we sat for four hours in Cousin Esther's house. The clock ticked. There were epic, Pinteresque pauses broken only by a crackle from the peat-burning fire. Men in flat caps and collarless shirts joined our group. Though conversation was thin, our hosts seemed not to mind. They loved doing nothing even more than we did. They were contented and comfortable in their goodness. If somebody said something jolly, there would be a burst of laughter followed by an even longer longueur of silence.

I contemplated this rustic, religious milieu.

It was all very mysterious. The fact that these individuals shared their roots and DNA with Betty seemed preposterous and implausible. My mother must surely be some kind of alien replicant from Planet Tart or a strange changeling.

I could imagine her as a child staring out at the misty peat bogs, longing for the nylons and high heels of the big city. Longing to get away from all this sensible goodness. Longing to primp. Longing for silks and satins. Longing to tart herself up.

We leave before teatime. We are trying to be polite. It is that baroque constipated politeness which is common to northern climes. It would have been rude to stay too long; this would have obliged our hosts to ask us if we wanted to stay for tea. They probably wanted us to stay for tea, but asking us would, in turn, have placed an obligation on us. If they invited us to stay for tea and we were not able to, then we would have had to endure the agony of declining, and they would have rued the day they set the whole thing in motion by asking us to stay for tea.

This insane game of snakes and ladders—a intricate circuit diagram of unspoken communication and wacky übergentility—made me wish we were Italian.

At the time of this visit, Italian culture was starting to penetrate the British Isles and my consciousness. The *Ciao! Ciao! Mangia! Mangia!* of Italian life seemed like the opposite of not asking somebody to stay for tea in case they were unable to comply. Italians knew how to cook and entertain. Italians knew how to dress. Italians knew how to tart themselves up.

Italian movie stars of the 1960s represented to my burgeoning sensibilities the ne plus ultra of stylish tarted-up glamour. I spent an inordinate amount of time wishing that I was Virna Lisi, wiggling down the Spanish Steps in a chic Pucci dress—or, better yet, riding down on the back of a tomato red Vespa—and throwing myself in the Trevi Fountain in full view of my adoring fans and frantically snapping paparazzi. *Ciao, Roma!*

Even their names were gorgeous: Claudia Cardinale, Silvana Mangano, Anna Magnani, Gina Lollobrigida. No self-respecting Italian chick would ever allow herself to be called something like Judi Dench or Kate Hudson.

Like my mother Betty, these stars and starlets were a great mixture of tarty and classy. Two words: Sophia Loren. Case closed.

Sophia and her ilk raised the bar on our notions of voluptuous, tarted-up femininity, leaving everyone else, with the possible exception of Brigitte Bardot and Marilyn Monroe, in the dust. Ballsy, busty, and fiery, they have no peer among today's red-carpet chippies. Come back to the five-and-dime, Monica Vitti, Monica Vitti!

We took a taxi back to Antrim. During the ride the adults began to revert to type. My grandfather removed his teeth and stuck them in his pocket. Betty began to re-Bettify herself with a spritz of *L'air du Temps*. She lit up a cigarette and reapplied her lipstick.

Complaining that they all needed a drink, the adults disappeared into a pub. My sister and I guzzled lemonade outside and practiced the fine art of doing nothing for an hour.

When she emerged, Betty was more like her old self again.

She had clearly spent time in the ladies' room. I was hugely relieved to see that she had begun the process of retarting herself. The sensible head scarf was gone. The nails were still unpainted, but bracelets and the mascara were back. With her customary aplomb, she had turned her sweater back to front. She had reaffirmed her commitment to eccentric glamour, and she looked all the better for it.

*   *   *

As I think back on that long-lost afternoon with the good people—my people!—of Antrim, I feel a tinge of sadness. I feel waves of regret for what might have been. What would have happened if Betty had not detarted herself for the occasion? What would the good people have made of the real Betty, the flashy, fabulously idiosyncratic Betty, as opposed to the depressing, inhibited, unrecognizable mutant who sat eating scones by their fire, desperately pretending she wasn't jonesing for a nicotine fix?

There's no doubt in my mind that they would have really liked her. She would have lit up their afternoon with her style and her brassy urban sophistication and left them jonesing for another visit. And now it's too late. They are all long gone.

For this missed opportunity I cannot help but blame Betty herself.

This was not Betty's finest hour. Far from it. By lowering the banner of eccentric glamour, even for that one afternoon, she did the universe a horrible disservice and committed what was in many ways a crime, albeit a minor one, against humanity.

For a contemporary example of this brand of folly, one need not look farther than Angelina. Yes, I'm talking about the Miss Jolie.

Why is it that, whenever she heads off to Africa or Vietnam to visit those less fortunate than herself, she does a total Betty. She always insists on shedding her Hollywood glamour and subjecting the underprivileged people of the world to a strange deglamorized version of herself. Where is the maquillage and where, more important, is that leather halter dress when it's most needed? If the most deprived people on earth don't deserve full-throttle movie star Angelina, then who does?

Why is she depriving the very people who are in such dire need? By dressing down she is violating the human rights of the very people she hopes to protect.

And Madonna is just as bad. Which of us has not gasped with uncomprehending shock at those earnest "children's author" outfits? You know the ones I'm talking about: the knee-length shift dresses and pastel cardigans. Whenever the great Madge launches one of her books, our lady of the whips and cone-bras looks like a depressed missionary.

Madge, you better watch your back. Those little brats are not as dumb as you think. They can see straight through those choreographed attempts at wholesomeness.

My fantasy is to dress myself up as a child—given my lack of height, this is not beyond the bounds of possibility—infiltrate one of her book signings and, when the moment is right, yell, "Hey, lady! What happened to the fishnets and spangled corsets?"

Angelina and Madonna have regal obligations, and so, now that you have graduated from the Academy of Eccentric Glamour, do you.

Noblesse oblige!

Your subjects are depending on you. Gird up your loins! Grab your scepter! Polish up your orb! And if, upon leaving your abode, you find that your doorman fails to comment upon your general magnificence, don't get in a snit. Look upon it as a compliment. If he is taking your eccentric glamour for granted, this is an indication that you have already successfully raised the bar. If, on the other hand, he is simply ignoring you, then run back upstairs and change into something insanely more fabulous.

Long live eccentric glamour!

Isabella Blow

The glamorous eccentric who got away

Immediately prior to finishing this book in the late spring of 2007, I placed several calls to Isabella Blow. It seemed churlish to hand in my text without at least a cursory conversation with the woman generally acknowledged by fashion insiders to be the Nancy Cunard/Peggy Guggenheim/Millicent Rogers/Marchesa Casati/Ottoline Morrell of our time. Isabella Blow may not have been a well-known name, but she was, at least as far as the cognoscenti were concerned, the reigning queen of glamorous eccentrics.

Why had I waited so long to approach Miss Blow? Why the reticence? Any woman who wore Philip Treacy hats shaped like lobsters and ships and never left the house without being dressed head to foot in surrealist couture clearly deserved inclusion in this oeuvre.

In hindsight, I realize my reluctance stemmed from reverse

snobbery: Why give prominence to a pampered aristocrat? The populist in me—he's an irate little chav with missing teeth who lives near my spleen—was determined to keep the focus on those self-invented, self-styled gals who were *not* on Karl Lagerfeld's Christmas card list. I was, in other words, discriminating against what I assumed was an undeserving bastion of moneyed privilege.

My populist approach was very conscious and stemmed from a lifetime of navigating the follies and self-referential foibles of la mode. The often exclusionary world of fashion is filled with high school notions of "in" and "out." It is driven by a desperate desire to draw lines in the sand and identify the stuff that was once so groovy and can now be gazed upon with contempt because it is over. But take an objective look at the world of fashion and you will immediately see that it is all 100 percent subjective. One person's Balenciaga is another person's Quacker Factory.

While certain people are more gifted than others in their ability to execute the craft of fashion—contemporary examples include Alber Elbaz, Olivier Theyskens, Narciso Rodriguez, and Isabel Toledo—the fact remains that, at the end of the day, it's all a matter of opinion and context. If you don't believe me, try wearing a John Galliano Dior topiary confection to a Chelsea gallery art opening and *then* hop over to New Jersey and wear it to the Secaucus branch of Dunkin' Donuts.

The bona fide glamorous eccentric is an accepting populist who understands that on judgment day the hippest Marc Jacobs catwalk chick and the frowzy housewife in the bunny sweater are equals. If a gal really and truly has *le chien*, then she has no need to look down her nose at anyone.

As Andy Warhol said; "If everyone's not a beauty, then nobody is."

Back to Miss Blow.

I began to leave messages for Isabella in late February, early March. If I expected to get any phone time with her, I knew I would need to be persistent. A highborn party gal like Miss Blow would never make time to return the calls of a lowly commoner like me. She would be too busy shooting grouse with her fancy-pants chums, or quaffing champagne during endless couture fittings with Alexander McQueen. Or maybe she was lying under a massive cedar of Lebanon in the grounds of her country estate wearing vintage Zandra Rhodes and reading first editions of Aldous Huxley and Evelyn Waugh.

Her unresponsiveness only fueled my persistence. Gradually tenacity gave way to mild hostility. After leaving the umpteenth message, I began muttering things like, "So much for good breeding!" and "Call me back, you bloody Sloane Ranger!"

When I opened the newspaper on May 9 and read that the poor darling had died, I was stunned. More shocks were in store. I quickly discovered that my preconceived notions about Miss Blow's life could not have been more off the mark. Oh! The folly of judging a broad by her couture!

The reports of her last months on this planet painted a desperate picture. In place of that cavalcade of snooty self-absorption and country house grandeur there was only misery and, most shockingly, a crushing lack of cash. Long since disinherited, abandoned by her husband, diagnosed with ovarian cancer, Isabella's life—she was forty-eight when she died—had gone from magic to tragic to allegedly drinking weed-killer.

Just as I had been ignorant of her last struggles and her suicidal sufferings, I was also ignorant regarding the true scope of her accomplishments. Reading the scores of obits and profiles, I came to understand that the great Isabella was a down-to-earth woman of almost Vreelandesque influence and creativity. The list of models, photographers, and designers who were discovered and propelled to stardom by La Blow's unstinting support and patronage is truly astounding: From Juergen Teller to Stella Tennant to Julien Macdonald, the roster of Blow alumni is endless.

The week she died I was in the UK staying with my dad in a senior citizens' home in Brighton. On Tuesday, May 15, 2007, I seriously toyed with abandoning Terry Doonan for the day, jumping on the train to Gloucester, and paying my last respects to this incredible woman on whose answering machine I had left all those unrelentingly gnatlike, annoying messages.

"Maybe you should go," said Terrence Doonan. "She seemed like such a nice, good-natured trout."

When, the following day, I saw the outfits of the attendees—the capes, the plumed hats, the trains, the finery (and that was just the men)—I was glad I had not gone. Having no eccentric glam attire with me, I would have felt like a chav version of Agnes Gooch.

"If Isabella could have seen the glamorous send-off she got, she would never have killed herself," one funeral attendee told me upon returning to New York.

I have decided I like this daffy notion. For purely selfish reasons I wish La Blow could have somehow previewed her send-off in a magical crystal ball and changed her mind. Maybe then we could have chatted over tea and scones. My treat!

Instead I am left with the gnawing feeling that I missed out on someone truly exceptional and that the armies of eccentric glamour have lost an important general.

The best way to honor the memory of this fallen heroine is to keep the flame alive. Unfurl the banner of eccentric glamour every single day of your life and, in the name of Miss Blow, wave it at the neighbors until the neighbors start waving back.